A YEAR OF
PREPARATION

WORLD YOUTH DAY '93
RESOURCE MANUAL

© 1992 WORLD YOUTH DAY, INC

*The International Gathering
of Young Adults and Youth*

With great enthusiasm the Catholic Church throughout the world prepares for the World Youth Day '93 Gathering in Denver, Colorado. This is a graced opportunity to invite young people to a deeper relationship with Christ in the Church and to promote the renewal of faith, zeal, and unity.

In a June 1992 message, the U.S. bishops called for a period of preparation for young adults and youth through parish programs, schools, universities, and families. This resource manual is a compendium of ideas to assist in this preparation.

This present document, *A Year of Preparation,* was prepared by Mark Pacione and Fr. Alfred McBride in collaboration with the staff of World Youth Day, the USCC Department of Education, and the NCCB Secretariat for Family, Laity, Women, and Youth. The text has been reviewed and approved by the ad hoc Committee for World Youth Day '93 and is authorized for publication by the undersigned.

Monsignor Robert N. Lynch
General Secretary,
September 21, 1992   NCCB/USCC

Cover photo: Denver Metro & Convention Bureau

ISBN 1-55586-528-3

Acknowledgments

This resource manual for the World Youth Day - 1993 Celebration has been made possible through many individual kindnesses and services. We wish to acknowledge the following; the Department of Education, Sr. Lourdes Sheehan, Fr. William Davis, Fr. John Pollard, Fr. Charles Hagan, and especially Sr. Elaine McCarron for her guidance; Fr. Al McBride who was the editor for the catechetical sections; the Secretariat for Family, Women, Laity, and Youth and the staff for World Youth Day Incorporated, especially Ms. Dolores Leckey, Ms. Terry Crovato, Ms. Sheila Garcia, Mr. Paul Henderson, Mr. Rick McCord and Mr. Mark Pacione; Mr. Ted Keene from the Archdiocese of Denver Office of Youth Ministry, Mr. Joe Mattingly from the Newman Center at Iowa State University, Ms. Marina Herrera for translation services, Fr. Michael Walsh, Fr. Ronald Krisman, Msgr. Alan Detscher, Ms. Donna Ashaka, Ms. Beverly Carroll, and Mr. Ron Cruz for assistance with reviewing. Thanks are also extended to the authors of the essays contained in the book, to the Bishops' Ad Hoc Committee on World Youth Day, to the World Youth Day Steering Committee, and to the USCC Office for Publishing and Promotion Services for its assistance in publishing this manual.

Note to Pastors, Principals, and Campus Leaders

This manual has been designed for parish and campus adult leaders in preparing for the International Meeting in Denver and developing plans and programs for the special year of outreach and evangelization. The manual should be shared with the director of Religious Education or chairperson of the Theology Department; the director of Campus Ministry, Youth Ministry and/or Young Adult Ministry; the director of Liturgy; and other pastoral leaders. The material from this book with the exception of the photographs may be reproduced.

CONTENTS

INTRODUCTION

A Brief History

At the conclusion of the Holy Year in 1984, Pope John Paul II invited young people from throughout the world to be present in Rome for the concluding Mass. During the ceremony he gave the Cross of the Holy Year to the young people as a reminder to them of their faith and redemption.

The following year, 1985, the Holy Father again invited young people to Rome, on Palm Sunday, this time for the observance of the United Nations International Year of Youth. That year many U.S. youth joined young people from the world in Rome to celebrate their faith and their youth. Few realized that this marked the start of a wonderful tradition.

The Holy Father's meeting with young people and his special letter to them in conjunction with the U.N. observance have led to yearly celebrations. Since 1985, Pope John Paul II has issued a letter to the youth of the world annually, and on alternating years he has invited the world's young people to meet with him at a special location for catechesis, fellowship, worship, and renewal. Such meetings have taken place in Rome (1985), Buenos Aires (1987), Santiago de Compostela (1989) and Czestochowa (1991).

On Palm Sunday, 1992, the Holy Father announced that the next international meeting for WYD would be held in the United States from August 11-15 in Denver, Colorado. In conjunction with the announcement, the cross, which had been entrusted to the young people in 1984, was given to a group of youth and young adults from the United States. This cross will be transported throughout the United States in preparation for World Youth Day '93 and is to arrive in Denver in August of 1993 as a symbol of our own pilgrimage of faith.

World Youth Day in the United States

In the United States the celebration of WYD has developed slowly. At first, the yearly observance took place on Palm Sunday, marked primarily by a Mass with the bishop in the cathedral. In 1988, the Administrative Committee of the National Conference of Catholic Bishops chose a different date for the U.S. celebration, hoping to encourage more parishes and schools to participate and to avoid conflict with Palm Sunday and Holy Week preparations. After consultation, the thirtieth Sunday in Ordinary Time, which is typically the last Sunday of

(Mark Pacione)

October, was chosen for the appropriateness of the lectionary readings and the lack of conflict with other national celebrations/observances.

In the past, the U.S. celebration of WYD has focused primarily on adolescents, those in junior high and high school. However, in Europe and in many other parts of the world, this day is primarily a celebration for college students and young adults. With the 1993 celebration, U.S. church leaders hope to expand WYD's emphasis to include college students and young adults.

Today, World Youth Day is typically celebrated on the 30th Sunday in Ordinary Time with some dioceses having celebrations on Palm Sunday, which initiates year-long observances concluding with parish and school activities at the end of October. No matter when WYD is celebrated, what is important is that it be celebrated throughout every diocese. For today, more than ever, young people need the support and affirmation of parents and the local community.

In January of 1991 the bishops of the U.S. released a message, *Putting Children and Families First*, asking all Catholics, indeed all families, churches, schools, governments to place children and youth first when it comes to spending time, resources, and energy. World Youth Day can be a day of affirming the talents and gifts of young people to welcome them and their participation in our lives and that of our Church and society.

Paul Henderson
Associate Director
Secretariat for Family, Women, Laity, and Youth

· · · · ·

1

GETTING STARTED

A Year of Preparation and Pilgrimage!

The World Youth Day '93 Gathering is a celebration for young adults, college students, and adolescents. In their statement about the World Youth Day '93 Gathering, the National Conference of Catholic Bishops called for "a special year of preparation characterized as a time of prayer and evangelization with an emphasis on reaching out to young people, both young adults and adolescents, particularly to those who are troubled, poor, vulnerable, and most in need of care." So while the actual gathering will happen August 11-15, 1993, our parishes and schools are called to start praying and preparing in January.

A parish or school can begin by organizing a World Youth Day Planning Team. The team should include youth and young adults. Other team members might include: young adult ministers, catechists, campus ministers, liturgists, RCIA team members, teachers, directors of religious education, parents, and youth ministers. It should be sensitive to the participation of minority populations. The WYD planning team can then work in the following areas:

Catechetical Efforts: to plan sessions for Catholic school religion classes, parish youth ministry programs, parish religious education programs, campus ministry events, young adult gatherings, retreats/day of reflection, etc.

Family Involvement: to involve families in prayer and preparation of the WYD Gathering, particularly if they have a member traveling to Denver.

Prayer and Worship: to coordinate prayer experiences for the community and the pilgrims in conjunction with the school or parish liturgy committee.

Participation in Pilgrimage: to organize the persons who will be traveling to Denver to best utilize the pilgrimage experience.

Evangelization Efforts: to implement a plan for intentional outreach to young adults and youth.

Service Efforts: to involve youth and young adults in service to the local community as preparation for the WYD Gathering.

This special year of preparation could be the time for a school or parish to breath new life into their outreach and ministry to youth and young adults. It can also be a time for parishes and schools to begin ministry programs if they have little or no organized effort in this area. (Two articles in the "Outreach" and "Evangelization" sections offer ideas for beginners.)

The entire resource manual, which is geared for parish, school, and campus leaders, has been printed on perforated pages for easy duplication and to facilitate sharing material among staff. While some articles are written for a specific target group, most of the ideas are adaptable to other age groups. We hope that you will make use of the entire manual as you prepare with your community for the WYD Gathering.

The World Youth Days and Gatherings are *providential opportunities to break our journey for a while*: they enable young people to examine their deepest aspirations, to heighten their sense of belonging to the Church, to proclaim their common faith in the Crucified and Risen Christ with increasing joy and courage. The provide an opportunity for many young people to make bold and enlightened choices which can help steer the future course of history under the powerful but gentle guidance of the Holy Spirit.

Pope John Paul II
World Youth Day Message 1993

• • • • •

A TIME LINE FOR WORLD YOUTH DAY PREPARATION

Early Preparations

CTNA World Youth Day Update Teleconference: Wednesday, October 21, 3:00-4:00 p.m. ET. Unscrambled.

Organize a planning team involving the pastoral council, school boards, and other leadership groups.

Begin to publicize for the meeting in Denver (August 11-15, 1993).

Make arrangements for transportation and housing. Identify which hub cities you will stop at if you are driving (bus or car).

Review the materials mailed by WYD '93 to all parishes and Catholic colleges and WYD information received from the arch/diocese.

If your parish or school does not have a young adult or youth ministry program, consider starting a program.

Distribute registration, housing, and health forms to the youth and young adults. Ask that deposits for trip to Denver be given by January 1 or sooner.

November-December

Plan an appropriate kick off for the special year of preparation around January 1, 1993.

Incorporate catechetical materials into already existing religious education programs for youth and young adults. Materials from the 1992 World Youth Day Manual are also designed to assist you in your preparation for 1993.

Set up fund raising activities to help with costs for the pilgrimage.

Begin having young adults/youth send in deposits/ registration forms.

January - Year of Outreach; Preparation Begins!

Organize a plan for service to the community by young adults and youth.

Plan intentional outreach/evangelization efforts for young adults and youth.

Help the community begin to hear the message of World Youth Day with articles in newsletters and bulletins on the theme of Jn 10:10.

Begin to pray for World Youth Day's success in the Prayer of the Faithful.

Suggest a registration deadline for preregistration by January 1, including deposits and the solidarity fee. Parishes and schools should turn in registration materials and fees to the arch/diocesan contact person by early February.

Share preparation plans with Parish Pastoral Council, School Board, and other appropriate leadership groups.

Distribute ideas for family participation in the preparation for WYD.

Gather youth and young adults interested in making the pilgrimage for prayer, community building, and planning.

Begin outreach/evangelization efforts directed to the young adults and youth of the parish, schoo,l or campus.

February - March

Distribute copies of the Youth Prayer and the Parents/Family Prayer for World Youth Day.

Introduce World Youth Day Theme Song to parish, school, or campus community.

Begin service to the community.

Enable arch/dioceses to send in registration materials and fees to the World Youth Day Denver office by March 15. Registration will continue through June, 1993.

April

Have a retreat/day of reflection using the sessions in the World Youth Day resource book.

Gather parents and families of those making the pilgrimage for an evening of prayer and information sharing.

Initiate a buddy system for those who have been welcomed back through the outreach/evangelization efforts.

May-June

At a liturgical celebration, pledge prayer and support for those who will be traveling to Denver.

Place meditations on the Easter Season Gospels in the bulletin or newsletters.

Sponsor an Abundant Life Festival for the parish during this Easter Season.

Continue outreach and evangelization efforts.

Continue service to community.

July

Have final meeting for pilgrimage delegation.

Initiate a prayer network that will cover every day through the end of the pilgrimage.

August

Have a send off celebration for the parish or school delegation.

Come to Denver, stopping at one of the hub cities or shrines that will welcome pilgrims.

Invite families of those on the pilgrimage to a special evening prayer during the World Youth Day Gathering. In Denver stop at the Cathedral of the Immaculate Conception to thank God for a safe pilgrimage.

Prepare an appropriate welcome home reception.

September

Invite young adults and youth to speak to the community while the experience is fresh.

Plan a reunion/pot luck dinner for the families of those who traveled to Denver.

Incorporate the themes of the special year of preparation in your Catechetical Sunday celebrations.

October

Organize a Homecoming Sunday for young adult and youth who may not have been active in the parish.

Organize a Homecoming Liturgy to coincide with

Homecoming Week to remind students that Jesus always welcomes us.

Use World Youth Day, 30th Sunday in Ordinary Time, October 24, 1993, to draw the special year of preparation to a close.

November

Have the World Youth Day planning team evaluate the year and refer any follow- up activity to the appropriate individuals or groups (pastor, student council, campus minister, parish youth ministry team, etc.)

Additional Information

Diocesan WYD Contacts

Each diocese across the United States has identified a person to serve as the contact for all World Youth Day information and registration. In planning for your young adults and youth to make the pilgrimage to Denver, work through the diocesan contact. In addition, your diocesan WYD contact will know about diocesan celebrations and gatherings in preparation for WYD. We strongly urge that all cultures be involved in the planning and programing.

Pilgrimage Hub Cities

To help people on their way to Denver, a network of hub cities has been established. Pilgrims will be able to request food and lodging at these cities on their way to and from Denver. The diocesan WYD contact will have information about making reservations at hub cities. As of September 5, 1992 hub cities include Boise, Idaho; Indianapolis, Indiana; Omaha, Nebraska; Salt Lake City, Utah; Rapid City, South Dakota; Witchita, Kansas; Salina, Kansas; Albuquerque, New Mexico; and San Antonio, Texas. Other cities may be added as necessary.

Holy Year Cross

At the end of the jubilee Holy Year in 1984, the Holy Father gave a special cross to the youth of the world that has since become a sign of the unity of young Catholics and the abundant life of Christ. This same cross was given to a group of young people from the United States on Palm Sunday, April 12, 1992. As part of the national preparation for World Youth Day, the cross will be brought to sites throughout the United States. It is possible that the Holy Year Cross will be in your area. It has been part of International Gatherings of the pope with young people in Rome (1985), Buenos Aires (1987), Santiago de Compostela (1989), and Czestochowa (1991). In 1993 the Holy Year Cross will be carried into Denver for the International Gathering there. For information concerning the place to which the Holy Year Cross will be brought, contact the National WYD office at 1-202-541-3001.

· · · · ·

SOME PERSPECTIVES TO REMEMBER IN YOUR PLANNING

Several themes and perspectives are key to a good celebration of World Youth Day. Please keep them in mind as you do your planning.

Evangelization and Service. The U.S. bishops have asked that the year of preparation be marked by evangelization and service. Help youth and young adults learn the skill of outreach and evangelization to their peers. Encourage young people to remain active in service to the community, especially service that reflects the abundant life that Jesus is for us. A special outreach can be extended to those young people who are troubled, poor, and most in need of love.

Multicultural Inclusiveness. National and international programs such as World Youth Day are unique opportunities to include experiences from other cultures in our programs. While we are continually striving to help all believers re-establish their familiarity with their own cultural roots, we should take advantage of this time to help our local communities understand and appreciate the gifts of other cultures. When we think about the racism that is still present in many ways, it is hard to imagine that we could spend too much time on cross-cultural experiences.

Pilgrimage. Physical journey and prayer naturally enhance each other. Take advantage of this moment by helping young adults and youth to understand the tradition of pilgrimage. Pilgrimages mark spiritual moments in our faith journey and celebrate our meeting with God in day to day living and culminate in our arriving at a holy place. For more about pilgrimage see page 5.

Family. It is fortunate that the WYD year of preparation is situated close to the publication in 1991 of the bishop's document, *Putting Children and Families First: The Challenge for our Church, Nation, and World,* The National Black Catholic Congress held in 1992 (the theme of which was The African American Family), and the United Nation's proclamation that 1994 will be the International Year of the Family. World Youth Day preparations should be sensitive to family systems and responsive to family needs.

Church as a Welcoming Community to Youth and Young Adults. If young adults and youth do not feel welcome in our parish, campus, and school communities during this year of preparation for World Youth Day, will they ever feel welcome? Enable youth and young adults to be visible in the local community. Give them opportunities to contribute and shape parish or campus life. Most important, involve youth and young adults in planning for World Youth Day. The year of preparation provides an excellent opportunity for the parish and campus to begin ministry to and with young adults and youth where little or none is present.

World Youth Day also challenges the older adults of the Church to discover the giftedness of young adults and youth. Young people have much to share with the Church and society and older persons must be open to discovering their gifts.

Be Good Stewards of the Earth. In planning be conscious of preserving the earth's resources, being gentle on the land and kind to its inhabitants.

Mark Pacione
World Youth Day
Preparation Programs Coordinator

· · · · ·

PILGRIMAGE AND WORLD YOUTH DAY

It is a 1990's pilgrimage, with sneakers replacing sandals and modern transportation replacing camel and horse. I expect many young people will come by foot and bike. Whatever way they travel, young people will encounter God in the near timeless mountains.

Archbishop William Keeler
Baltimore

Pilgrim, Pilgrimage. . .these are words that carry different meanings for different people. In the United States those who emigrated from Europe connect the word pilgrim to our heritage. Plymouth Rock and Thanksgiving symbolize and celebrate the Pilgrims who came across the Atlantic Ocean seeking new life in a new world. Our ancestors who were part of the westward expansion also used the word pilgrim to describe those establishing new homesteads in frontier lands. Our Native American ancestors will remember pilgrim from a different perspective and

may see the European pilgrim as one whose expansion was at their expense. For some tribes, pilgrimage evokes the painful image of forced resettlement. Theologians speak about a pilgrim church and refer to believers as pilgrim people. We pass through this world as pilgrims on a pilgrimage to the promise of eternal life. Christians have a rich tradition of pilgrimage to many different holy places and shrines but they are not alone. Both Moslems and Jews also place high value on the tradition of a pilgrimage.

In preparing for World Youth Day, we should be attentive to the pilgrimage component. While the destination of a pilgrimage is most often a church, shrine, or other special place that manifests God's presence, the pilgrimage to Denver will have an additional focal point. All those traveling to Denver will be invited to make a pilgrimage to the Cathedral of the Immaculate Conception. But for the first time the international gathering will not take place at an historical pilgrimage site. Rather, the shrine will arise from the pilgrimage. Our pilgrimage to Denver will emphasize that the human being is the true sanctuary, the true shrine of God. Denver, therefore, is not a pilgrimage to a shrine but a pilgrimage of the shrines. World Youth Day pilgrims will be making their pilgrimage to the sanctuary of the human person. Most certainly, God is manifested in the hearts of young people who will gather in faith at the foot of the mountains of Colorado.

A pilgrim always encounters something new on a pilgrimage and, therefore, leaves something behind. This pilgrimage is one which can emphasize the

(Paul Henderson)

5

leaving behind of the past, of the worldly values, to embrace the new evangelization, the heavenly values. A pilgrimage is always a penitential journey toward the Eucharist. A pilgrimage therefore, is always catechetical and sacramental. It is a reflection on history, culture, pedagogy, biblical themes, and above all the sacraments of reconciliation and of the Eucharist. When designing prayer experiences for your pilgrimage, look at Psalms 121 through 125. These psalms are traditional hymns that were sung by pilgrims on their way to Jerusalem.

In your preparations for your World Youth Day Pilgrimage, remember to:

1. Teach about pilgrimage. While there are many different concepts, we need World Youth Day participants to understand our Catholic tradition.

2. Give folks an opportunity to participate in a pilgrimage locally. Not only would a local pilgrimage be helpful in preparing participants for their experience in Denver, but it would also be an opportunity for youth and young adults to continue their personal spiritual renewal after they return home.

3. Make your trip to Denver a pilgrimage not a convention. We are a pilgrim people on a journey to be near our God. Take advantage of hub cities and shrines that you might meet along your travel route. Include prayer and the struggle of travel in your planning.

. . . . .

THE MEANING OF PILGRIMAGE

By Fr. Anthony Czarnecki
USCC Migration Refugee Services

The word *pilgrimage* may sound foreign to contemporary generations in the United States. Today, people are more familiar with activities and movements such as the March for Life, walk-a-thons, parades, and vacation trips as tourists. A pilgrimage is an entirely different experience. One can understand pilgrimage as a journey undertaken for spiritual motives to a church or some other sacred place. The elements essential to a pilgrimage include:

Spiritual Motivation. Spiritual motivation is an essential part of a pilgrimage. The individual makes a decision to undertake a pilgrimage for a spiritual purpose, such as gratitude to God for graces received, atoning for sins, personal conversion, and/or for reasons of devotion. In this way, a pilgrimage

greatly differs from tourism. Tourists take in the sights with their eyes while pilgrims take in the experience with their hearts. A pilgrimage is, above all, a striving for a closer unity with our triune God - Father, Son, and Holy Spirit - it means enduring some form of hardship, suffering, and tediousness for the sake of interior personal growth.

The Journey. Some form of movement always accompanies a pilgrimage, and it involves all sorts of travel, not just walking. To go away, to change your daily surrounding and routines, and to visit a different place has not only psychological but also significant spiritual meaning. Quite often, Jesus took his disciples to out-of- the way places for rest and meditation, where he shared with them the mysteries of the kingdom.

Customarily, a pilgrimage is envisioned as a group of people walking to one common destination. An individual pilgrimage is also very common. Along the journey, people follow a certain ritual of prayer, reflection, and singing. A pilgrimage itself is enriched by personal discovery, as is exemplified in Scripture by the two disciples on the road to Emmaus. Walking together, sharing, and praying create a sense of community. A pilgrimage is not something totally abstracted from the life of the Church, neither is it totally complete in itself or finished once this particular journey has ended. One's whole life is a pilgrimage to God.

Sacred Site. The destination of the pilgrimage is almost always a church or other sacred place in which it is believed that God's presence is manifested in a special way. Pilgrimages are often conducted to places associated with the life of Christ (e.g. the Holy Land), the Blessed Mother, or the lives of the saints. These places are called shrines and at them people encounter the presence of God in a very personal way.

Since the gathering in Rome for the U.N. International Year of Youth in 1985, a spirit of pilgrimage has been part of WYD international gatherings. The pilgrimage experience in Europe, Central and South America, French Canada, to name a few places is part of regular church life. The value of a pilgrimage, its connectedness with everyday life, and its impact on an individual and community can be further developed in the United States. In fact, among different cultural or ethnic groups within our country, pilgrimages to particular shrines are already flourishing.

Spiritual assistance will be offered at various shrines across the country for those journeying to Denver. The spirit of hospitality and welcome which the young people will experience at these shrines will certainly intensify the spirit of their pilgrimage.

To ensure that the journey to Denver will be a true pilgrimage, special preparation is needed. A pilgrimage does not start the day one begins to travel, but requires a strategy of preparation and the cooperation of all those involved.

World Youth Day activities for 1993 will include a pilgrimage experience. Various routes will be designated to give young people from across the world an opportunity to make a pilgrimage to shrines on the way to Denver and to the Cathedral of the Immaculate Conception in Denver itself. There also will be a pilgrimage on Saturday, August 14, 1993 from the various catechetical sites to the site of the Saturday evening vigil; Sunday Mass with the pope will be held. It is recommended that young people prepare both spiritually and physically for their pilgrimage. Further information can be provided by your diocesan World Youth Day contact person.

Pilgrimage of the Cross

The 1993 World Youth Day in Denver presents us with a unique opportunity to introduce the pilgrimage experience to our young people as a preparation for their encounter with the Holy Father and pilgrims from around the world.

To facilitate this experience, the Holy Year Cross will itself be transported about and be available to dioceses throughout the United States. A special ritual has been developed to prepare for the presence of the cross in your diocese and to promote subsequent activities related to World Youth Day. To obtain further information on the relationship of the cross to your community, please call the World Youth Day office at 1-202-541-3001.

In our view the pilgrimage may well be the expression, the occasions, and, as it were, the synthesis of all (our pentential) practices which have as their crown the celebration of the Eucharist. In the genuine tradition of Christian asceticism, pilgrimages have always had devotion and expiation as their motives. The pilgrimage can still today be inspired by the same motives. . . . It is essential that the mark of a pilgrimage, besides prayer and penance, be the practice of love of neighbor. For that is a clear proof of love for God and it must be expressed in spiritual and corporal works of mercy towards those most in need . . . .

Pope Paul VI
Iniziandosi ufficialmente
May 31, 1973

· · · · ·

AN INTERNATIONAL GATHERING OF YOUNG ADULTS & YOUTH

(Gary Allen Brown)

MESSAGE OF THE HOLY FATHER

TO THE YOUTH OF THE WORLD ON THE OCCASION OF THE VIII WORLD YOUTH DAY - 1993

"I came so that they might have life and have it more abundantly."

Dear Young People!

1. Following our meetings in Rome, Buenos Aires, Santiago de Compostela, and Czestochowa, our pilgrimage through contemporary history continues. The next stop will be in Denver, in the heart of the United States, in the Rocky Mountains of Colorado, where in August 1993 the Eighth World Youth Day will be celebrated. Together with many young Americans, young people from every nation will gather together, as on previous occasions, as if to symbolize the living faith, or at least the most urgent questions of the world of youth from five continents.

These regular celebrations are not meant to be mere rituals, justified merely by the fact that they are repeated; in fact, they spring from a deep-seated need originating in the human heart and reflected in the life of the pilgrim and missionary church.

The World Youth Days and Gatherings are *providential opportunities to break our journey for a while:* they enable young people to examine their deepest aspirations, to heighten their sense of belonging to the Church, to proclaim their common faith in the Crucified and Risen Christ with increasing joy and courage. They provide an opportunity for many young people to make bold and enlighten choices which can help steer the future course of history under the powerful but gentle guidance of the Holy Spirit.

We are witnessing a 'succession of empires' in our world - the repeated attempts to create political unity which particular individuals have tried to impose on others. The results are there for all to see. True and lasting unity cannot be created by coercion and violence. It can only be achieved by building on the foundations of a common heritage of values accepted and shared by all, values such as respect for the dignity of the human person, a willingness to welcome life, the defence of human rights, and openness to transcendence and the realm of the spirit.

In view of this, and as a response to the challenges of our changing times, the World Youth Gathering is meant to be a *first step and a proposal of a new unity,* a unity which transcends the political order but enlightens it. It is based on awareness that only the Creator of the human heart can adequately satisfy its deepest yearnings. The World Youth Day is thus a proclamation of Christ who says to the men and women of our own century too: "I came that they might have life, and have it to the fullest." (Jn 10:10).

(CNS)

2. And so we come to the heart of the theme that will guide our reflections throughout this year of preparation for the next World Youth Day.

Different languages have different worlds to express what no one would ever wish to lose under any circumstances, what constitutes the expectation, longing and hope of all mankind. But there is no better world then "life" to sum up comprehensively the greatest aspiration of all humanity. "Life" indicates the sum total of all the goods that people desire, and at the same time what makes them possible, obtainable, and lasting.

Is not the history of mankind deeply marked by a frantic and tragic search for something or someone able to free it from death and guarantee life?

Human existence has its moments of crisis and weariness, despondency and gloom. Such a sense of dissatisfaction is clearly reflected in much of today's literature and films. In the lights of this distress, it is easier to understand the particular difficulties of adolescents and young people stepping out with uncertainty to encounter all the fascinating promises and dark uncertainties which are part of life.

Jesus came to provide the ultimate answer to the yearning for life and for the infinite which his Heavenly Father had poured into our hearts when he created us. At the climax of revelation, the Incarnate Word proclaims, "I am the life" (Jn 14:6), and "I came that they might have life" (Jn 10:10). But what life? Jesus' intention was clear: *the very life of God*, which surpasses all the possible aspirations of the human heart (cf. 1 Cor 2:9). The fact is that through the grace of Baptism we are already God's children (cf. 1 Jn 3:1-2).

Jesus came to meet men and women, to heal the sick and the suffering, to free those possessed by devils and to raise the dead: he gave himself on the Cross and rose again from the dead, revealing that he is the Lord of life: the author and the source of life without end.

3. Our daily experience tells us that life is marked by sin and threatened by death, despite the desire for good which beats in our hearts and the desire for life which courses through our veins. However little heed we pay to ourselves and to the frustrations which life brings us, we discover that *everything within us impels us to transcend ourselves,* urges us to overcome the temptation of superficiality or despair. It is then that human beings are called to become disciples of that Other One who infinitely transcends them, in order to enter at last into true life.

There are also false prophets and false teachers of how to live. First of all there are those who teach people to leave the body, time and space in order to be able to enter into what they call 'true life.' They condemn creation, and in the name of a deceptive spirituality they lead thousands of young people along the paths of an impossible liberation, which eventually leaves them even more isolated, victims of their own illusions and of the evil in their own lives.

Seemingly at the opposite extreme, there are the teachers of the 'fleeting moment,' who invite people to give free rein to every instinctive urge or longing, with the result that individuals fall prey to a sense of anguish and anxiety leading them to seek refuge in false artificial paradises, such as that of drugs.

And there are those who teach that the meaning of life lies solely in the quest for success, the accumulation of wealth, the development of personal abilities, without regard for the needs of others or respect for values, at times not even for the fundamental value of life itself.

These and other kinds of false teachers of life, also numerous in the modern world, propose goals which not only fail to bring satisfaction but often intensify and exacerbate the thirst that burns in the human heart. Who then can understand and satisfy our expectations? Who but the One who is the Author of life can satisfy the expectations that he

himself has placed in our hearts? He draws close to each and every one of us in order to announce a hope that will never disappoint; he who is both the way and the life: *the pathway into life.*

Left to ourselves, we could never achieve the ends for which we have been created. Within us there is a promise which we find we are incapable of attaining. But the Son of God who came among us has given his personal assurance: "I am the way, and the truth, and the life" (Jn 14:6). As Saint Augustine so strikingly phrased it, Christ "wishes to create a place in which it is possible for all people to find true life." This `place' is his Body and his Spirit, in which the whole of human life, redeemed and forgiven, is renewed and made divine.

4. In fact, the life of each of us was thought of and willed by God before the world began, and we can rightly repeat with the Psalmist: "O Lord, you have probed me and you know me. . .truly you have formed my inmost being; you knit me in my mother's womb" (Ps 139).

This life, which was in God from the beginning (cf Jn 1:4). is a life which is freely given, which holds nothing back for itself and is freely and unstintingly communicated to others. It is light, "the real light, which gives light to every man" (Jn 1:9). It is God, who came to make his dwelling among us (cf Jn 1:14), to show us the path to the immortality belonging to the children of God, and to make it accessible to us.

In the mystery of his Cross and Resurrection, Christ has destroyed death and sin, and has bridged the infinite distance that separates all people from new life in him. "I am the resurrection and the life," he proclaims. "Whoever believes in me, though he should die, will come to life, and whoever is alive and believes in me will never die" (Jn 11:25).

Christ achieves all this by pouring out his Spirit, the giver of life, in the Sacraments; especially in Baptism, the Sacrament by which the fragile life which we receive from our parents and which is destined to end in death becomes instead a path to eternity; in the Sacrament of Penance which continually renews God's life within us by the forgiveness of sins; and in the Eucharist, the 'bread of life' (cf Jn 6:35), which feeds the 'living' and gives strength to their steps during their pilgrimage on earth, so that they can say with the Apostle Paul: "I still live my human life, but it is a life of faith in the son of God, who loved me and gave himself for me."

5. New life, the gift of the Risen Lord, then spreads far and wide, flowing into every sphere of human experience: the family, the school, the workplace, everyday activities and leisure time.

That new life begins to flower here and now. The sign of its presence and growth is love. As Saint

John tells us: "That we have passed from death to life we know because we love the brothers" (1 Jn 3:14) with a true love that is put into practice. Life flourishes in the gift of self to others, in accordance with each person's vocation- in the ministerial priesthood, in consecrated virginity, in marriage - so that all can share the gifts they have received, in a spirit of solidarity, especially with the poor and the needy.

The person who is "begotten from above" thus becomes able to "see the kingdom" of God (cf Jn 3:3), and to take part in building up social structures more worthy of every individual and of all humanity, in promoting and defending the culture of life against all threats of death.

6. Dear young people, you ask a question that many of your friends often put to you: How and where can we come to know this life? How and where can we live it?

You can find the answer by yourselves, if you really try to live faithfully in the love of Christ (cf Jn 15:9). Then you will personally experience the truth of those words of his: "I am. . . the life" (Jn 14:6) and you will be able to bring this joyful message of hope to everyone. Christ has made you his ambassadors, the primary evangelizers of your contemporaries.

The next World Youth Day in Denver will give us an ideal opportunity to reflect together on this theme of great interest to everyone. We must therefore prepare for this important meeting, first of all by looking around us to discover and as it were make a list of all the "places" where Christ is present as the source of life. They may be our parish communities, apostolic groups and movements, monasteries, convents and religious houses, but also the individual persons through whom — as the disciples at Emmaus

experienced — Christ is able to touch hearts and open them up to hope.

Dear young people, with a spirit of generous self-giving, recognize that you are directly involved in the new evangelization, which demands the involvement of all of us. Proclaim Christ, who "died for all, so that those who live might live no longer for themselves, but for him who for their sakes died and was raised up" (2 Cor 5:15).

7. You, dear young people of the United States who will be the hosts of the next World Youth Day, have been given the joy of welcoming as a gift of the Spirit this meeting with the many young men and women who will come to your country on pilgrimage from all over the world.

You are already making fervent spiritual and material preparations for this event, which involves each member of your ecclesial Communities.

It is my earnest hope that this extraordinary event will bring you ever greater enthusiasm and fidelity in following Christ and in joyfully welcoming his message, the source of new life.

I therefore entrust all of you to the Blessed Virgin Mary, through whom we have been given the Author of life, Jesus Christ, the Son of God and Our Lord. With great affection I send all of you my blessing.

From the Vatican, on 15th August 1992, the Solemnity of the Assumption of the Blessed Virgin Mary.

Joannes Paulus II

JOANNES PAULUS II

. . . . .

EVANGELIZATION

A CALL TO EVANGELIZATION

> . . . [Y]ou will be able to bring this joyful message of hope to everyone. Christ has made you his ambassadors, the primary evangelizers of your contemporaries.
>
> Pope John Paul II
> World Youth Day Address 1993

Evangelization is one of the primary tasks during this year of preparation for World Youth Day. This year of preparation and the gathering in Denver are a wonderful opportunity for evangelization. But can the Church throughout the United States take advantage of this very visible celebration and harness the energy of the World Youth Day celebration, using it to proclaim the gospels? Can we ride the energy of the World Youth Day celebration and use it to transform our world? The gospel roots and the challenges of evangelization are addressed in the National Conference of Catholic Bishops' document, *Heritage and Hope.* Although the letter was written as a statement on the Fifth Centenary of Evangelization in the Americas, the message is most appropriate for us as we prepare for World Youth Day.

Recommitment through Evangelization

What has happened to the hidden energy of the Good News that so moved Christians of the past? And to what extent and in what way is that evangelical force capable of really transforming our world today?

We proclaim Good News that is, first of all, the revelation that God the Almighty Creator is the loving Father of each of us, who ". . . so loved the world that he gave his only Son, so that everyone who believes in him might not perish but might have eternal life" (Jn 3:16).

The foundation, center, and summit of the Good News is the proclamation that in Jesus Christ salvation is offered as a gift of God's grace and mercy. We are each called to respond personally to that grace and mercy of Christ. We are challenged to experience a total interior renewal, a profound change of mind and heart that leads to a life lived in the spirit of the beatitudes. Christ's salvation exceeds the limits of this world and is fulfilled in union with

God forever in heaven. The Good News reveals that Christ has sent his Holy Spirit among us, that he has given us the Church through which we are called to relate to him personally, to experience and live out the way of life of his kingdom, to celebrate the Eucharist, to receive instruction, guidance, and sacramental graces that will fulfill our search for God and bring us to eternal happiness with him.

Through both Scripture and tradition Jesus has enriched his Church with the fullness of his teachings. The Good News reaches every part of human activity. It proclaims the rights and responsibilities of each human being. It addresses family life and life in society, calling us to strive for peace and justice and for the authentic advancement of humanity. It speaks of the dignity of work, of all human endeavors that are destined to complement the creating action of God in order to serve the human community. It challenges us to transform every aspect of the work place in light of the gospel. Evangelization means embracing the Good News. It means a conversion of hearts that begins with our own, whether we are clergy, religious, or laity.

It involves reaching out with the compassion of Christ to the alienated of our Church, reconciling the great number of people who have been lured from the Lord by contemporary materialism, secularism, and hedonism and offended by failures and insensitivity of their Christian communities. It includes reaching out to the unchurched and to those who do not share the fullness of our blessings as members of the Church of the Lord Jesus.

When we speak of evangelization, we are speaking of challenging not only individuals but also society at large to change. We are speaking of God's power to transform cultures, to renew political, economic, ecclesial, and human relationships.

The moment calls for Christians, faithful to the gospel, to realize the hope that a people renewed by the saving presence of Christ may help build a better society. May the new evangelization stimulate holiness, integrity, and tireless activity to promote the dignity of all human life, thus witnessing more fully to the presence of the kingdom of God in our midst. May we all, through a fresh commitment to the gospel, engage in a new *discovery,* a new creation of a world still being sought: a community of faith, a culture of solidarity, a civilization of love. The future is struggling to be born as the Word of God entreats men and women to respond more fully to its message. It is one in which a "new inspired synthesis of the spiritual and temporal, of the ancient and modern" might be brought forth.

All of the *People of God* must do their part in this new evangelization. *Scholars and teachers,* in reverence for the truth, should see their work as contributing to the good of humanity in the light of the gospel. *Parents,* in their trying but immeasurably important task, should work to build the *domestic church* in which faith and virtue are nurtured. The *young,* who have a special vocation to hope, should spread among their peers the message of light and life that is in Christ. *Artists,* who toil to create works of beauty and meaning, should view their art as a medium through which others may see something of the transcendent. *Public servants,* who struggle in an environment of utilitarianism, should spread the justice of Christ's kingdom by their way of life. *Laborers and mechanics,* those working in commerce and law, those who care for the sick, and those who engage in scientific research: the gospel calls them all to a special witness in our society. It calls each of us to incarnate the Good News of Christ the midst of our labors.

In *Heritage and Hope,* the bishops point out several of the challenges of evangelization. Here are some of them which will be helpful as we approach this World Youth Day celebration.

1. Be salt and light for the world, and at times, a sign of contradiction that challenges and transforms the world according to the mind of Christ.

2. Give examples of lives of faith, goodness and service.

3. Challenge publicly the conscience of society to uphold basic human values that advance fundamental human rights.

4. All Americans are encouraged to understand better the role of native peoples in our history and respond to the just grievances of our Native American brothers and sisters.

5. Reject all forms of racism.

6. Renew our appreciation of the multicultural beauty of our Church and our country and extend welcome to the new immigrants to our land: Asian, Europeans, Africans, and citizens of the Americas.

7. Strive for a new reconciliation in the spirit of the gospel among all Americans.

8. Right the evils of the past and the present and be forceful advocates of the peace and justice proclaimed by the gospel.

9. Share human and material resources with those

evangelizers of other lands who strive to bring the gospel to their peoples.

Dear young people, with a spirit of generous self-giving, recognize that you are directly involved in the new evangelization, which demands the involvement of all of us. Proclaim Christ, who "died for all, so that those who live might live no longer for themselves, but for him who for their sakes died and was raised up" (2 Cor. 5:15).

Pope John Paul II
World Youth Day Address 1993

• • • • •

YOUTH AND YOUNG ADULTS AS EVANGELIZERS

By Mark Bercham, N.E.T.

Circumstances invite us to make special mention of the young. Their increasing number and growing presence in society and likewise the problems assailing them should awaken in everyone the desire to offer them with zeal and intelligence the Gospel ideal as something to be known and lived. And on the other hand, young people who are well trained in faith and prayer must become more and more the apostles of youth. The Church counts greatly on their contribution.

On Evangelization in the Modern World
Pope Paul VI

Pope Paul VI in his Apostolic Exhortation, *Evangelii Nuntiandi,* calls attention to two important considerations for those of us who work with youth and young adults. First, they need to be evangelized. None of us will argue with that. We are all well aware of the many challenges facing our young people today. The voices of materialism, secularism, sexual promiscuity, drugs, and alcohol clamor for their attention and allegiance. The breakdown of many families and the loss of cultural supports for living a Christian life have left many young people with little or no faith experience or religious instruction.

Yes! It responds in our heart, youth and young adults need to be evangelized. Let's do it! But Pope Paul VI also shares something equally important when we consider evangelization. Young people themselves must be the evangelizers. Young people sharing the Gospel with other young people. That's not to say that adults don't have an important part to play. Parents are the first and primary teachers of their children in matters of faith. Priests, religious, and youth and young adult ministers all have a vital part to play in the work of youth evangelization. Indeed, the whole parish community is called to live a life of holiness and service that will attract and support young people in living a Catholic Christian life.

Why do youth have an important part to play in the Church's task of evangelizing young people?

Let me share with you what I see as the strengths of youth as evangelizers and what they need from us (adults) to succeed. There are four reasons why I think youth make great evangelizers.

First, they are zealous and idealistic. Young people still dream. They still believe the world can be better. They want to make a difference. As a young person encounters Christ and experiences his personal love, the excitement of new found faith coupled with youthful zeal produces a dynamism that is very attractive to other youth.

Second, youth and young adults make good evangelizers because they speak the language. They listen to other young people. Whether we like it or not, our young people look to and listen to their peers more than their parents. In their transition to adulthood, they are beginning to look less to mom and dad and more to their friends in answering some of life's questions. The opinions of their peers carry weight. I have seen a number of situations where one or two

faith-filled teenagers have brought a large number of their friends back to Christ and life in the Church.

Third, youth are effective in evangelizing other youth because they keep the message simple. All too often, we older folks make following the Lord too complex. We provide all sorts of religious instruction but neglect the simple message that Christ loves us and wants to be in a relationship with us. Don't get me wrong. Catechism is important, but the Christian life seems oppressive without experiencing the love and personal interest of the Lord. Young people don't provide theology. They share, "This is what Christ has done for me and he wants to be with you." Simple.

Fourth, the Bible and our tradition are full of illustrations of God using the young to spread his word and his work. The call of Jeremiah, "Say not, 'I am too young.' To whomever I send you, you shall go; whatever I command you, you shall speak." (Jer 1:7); and the call of Timothy, "Let no one look down on you because of your youth, but be a continuing example of love, faith, and purity to believers." (I Tm 4:12) are well known to us. In addition, saints such as Maria Goretti, Theresa of Lisieux, Francis of Assisi, Louis - King of France, Francis Xavier, Bernadette, Martin de Porres Catherine of Alexandria, Peter Claver, and Julia Billiart are examples of young women and men who gave their lives to God at a young age and were used by God to advance the kingdom.

What must we do to assist our young people in their call to evangelism?

First, we must provide them with opportunities to share their faith. Often we overlook the valuable

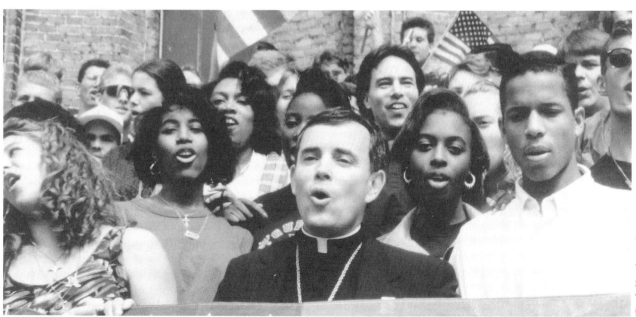

(Paul Henderson)

13

resource that our young people can be in our evangelization efforts. All too often we lose our most enthusiastic young people to nondenominational groups and movements which offer them numerous ways to make significant contributions in the work of spreading the Gospel. Forming retreat teams, music and drama troupes, student-led groups, mission trips to serve in poor areas, school bible studies, and prayer meetings are a few examples of ways that young people can make a significant impact.

Second, young people need practical instruction in how to live the Christian life. For any of us, young or old, to be effective evangelizers we must be growing in our own love and faith in God. As the oft used saying goes,"You can't give what you don't have." Most "on-fire" young people need help in how to pray, how to read the Bible, and how to understand the sacraments so that they can mature in their new found faith. They need practical instruction in relating as brothers and sisters, in serving others, in speaking of their experience, and in resolving conflict so that the witness of life matches their words.

Third, young people need to be trained in how to lead. Most young people are used to following, especially following the crowd. An evangelizer needs to lead. They need training in how to share their faith with confidence rather than fear. They must be taught how to listen to their friends' concerns without being judgmental and how to invite their friends to turn to Christ. They need support in taking a positive stand on issues that affect youth such as chastity, honesty in school and work, and resistance to peer pressures.

Fourth, young people who evangelize will need us to serve as a resource for them as they uncover other youth who are experiencing personal difficulties. My experience has been that as you begin sharing God's love and mercy with young people, they begin sharing their personal struggles with you. Youth evangelizers need to know where to turn when another youth shares that he/she has been abused or has attempted suicide. As the family system and the culture continues to deteriorate, young people's personal problems will continue to escalate. We must serve as a resource to our youth evangelizers so that they can help kids in need get plugged into a helping system.

As you can see, youth evangelizing youth doesn't get us adults off the hook. There is still a lot of work that we must do. But it's worth it. As we involve our young people in the work of evangelization, we will see them become more fully connected to Christ themselves. As you share your faith, your faith deepens. As young people do the work of the Church, they become more interested in the work of the Church. One of the things I never grow tired of hearing is a young person who tells me how excited he/she was as he/she shared his/her faith with another and suddenly realized, "God used me!"

. . . . .

EVANGELIZATION: A RELATIONAL RATIONALE FOR SPIRITUAL GROWTH

By J. David Stone

Youth Ministry Television Network

Was it a program or a person that brought you in touch with God? My hunch is that it was a person; someone who loved you anyway. Someone who did not have to love you. Someone who loved you unconditionally! When you are "there" for someone - acting in their interest, touching them where they hurt, being their friend in time of trouble, you are evangelizing - it's relational ministry.

Lifestyle Christianity

What does it mean to be a Christian? That was the question asked a panel of three ministers during a spiritual emphasis week at a small Christian college. I listened intently as the panel attempted to answer the question.

The first minister offered a stuffy response, "Being a Christian means to acquire knowledge of the Christ through God's Word, developing a ritualistic approach of communication with God, and acting on that knowledge with courage."

The next minister, in a tone and demeanor that would strike envy among today's television evangelists, said "To be a Christian is to be washed by the blood of the sacrificial lamb and cleansed forever in the temple of the Holy Spirit." Then he turned to the last member of the panel and asked, "Isn't that right, Reverend Bob?"

Bob was obviously the junior member of the panel of ministers and seemed surprised by the query. Bob blurted out: "I'm not sure I know what either one of you said. When I think of being a Christian, I simply recognize that God loves me and what a tremendous difference that love has made in my life." There was an eruption of thunderous applause and then a standing ovation of approval from the students.

Christianity is demonstrated by the way we live our lives. Evangelization is living in front of people in order to attract them by our lives rather than just by our creed.

Sister Thea Bowman, in response to how we could best "evangelize" young people, answered, "Just let 'em know you love them!" I relate to that. Showing God's love by the way we treat people is to take on the Christian armor. It communicates so much better than "telling people about the love of Jesus." That is not to say we should refrain from a verbal witness, but more that we should integrate a whole person approach - *walking the talk!*

When we *walk the talk,* we automatically shed the clothing of hypocrisy and *goodie two shoes.* The people we respect, high school leaders such as class officers, cheerleaders, athletes, and honor society members, earn that respect by who they are, not who they say they are. When we live our convictions out in front of the world, there is no greater witness, there is no greater peace of mind, and there is no greater evangelization. Jesus is our model, and he told us to "Go and make disciples of all nations."

Resources on Evangelization

Pope Paul VI, *On Evangelization in the Modern World* (*Evangelii Nuntiandi*), apostolic exhortation (Washington, D.C.: United States Catholic Conference, 1975), Pub. No. 129-6.

National Conference of Catholic Bishops, *Heritage and Hope: Evangelization in the United States,* English/Spanish text (Washington, D.C.: United States Catholic Conference, 1991), Pub. No. 386-8.

Evangelization in the Modern World: A Summary of the Apostolic Exhortation of Pope Paul VI (Washington, D.C.: Paulist National Catholic Evangelization Association).

John Paul II, *On the Vocation and Mission of the Lay Faithful in the Church and in the World* (*Christifidelis Laici*), (Washington, D.C.: United States Catholic Conference, 1989), Pub. No. 274-8.

The National Federation for Catholic Youth Ministry has produced a position paper on evangelization of young people titled, *Called to Be Witnesses and Storytellers.* This paper will provide primary direction for preparatory evangelization for World Youth Day 1993. It addresses Catholic youth evangelization in its foundations, principles, dynamics, and challenges. Published by the National Federation for Catholic Youth Ministry, Inc., as a companion to the *Challenge for Adolescent Catechesis,* it integrates evangelization and youth ministry and will be indispensable for the evangelization of Catholic youth through the 1990s. It will be available in early 1993. To order contact: NFCYM; 3700 A Oakview Terrace, N.E.; Washington, D.C. 20017. Voice 202-636-3825; FAX 202-526-7544.

World Youth Day gives us a unique opportunity to increase our outreach and evangelization efforts to young adults and youth. The World Youth Day resource manual for 1992, *Live the Faith, Share the Story!,* had several excellent articles on outreach and evangelization. In making your plans for this special year of preparation, you may want to refer especially to two of these articles: "Evangelization Training Session for Youths," pp. 13-15 and "Integrating Youths into the Parish," pp. 32-33. Both the 1992 and 1993 manuals have several resources to assist you in your efforts to invite young adults and youth to the church and to bring them the message of Christ's abundant life.

> We must look for new ways to reach our young people with the Good News of Jesus Christ and try to bring back those who feel alienated and isolated from our community.
>
> National Conference of Catholic Bishops World Youth Day Message, June 1992

· · · · ·

© 1992 WORLD YOUTH DAY, INC.

15

OUTREACH AND MINISTRY WITH YOUNG ADULTS AND YOUTH

WORKING DEFINITION OF YOUNG ADULT MINISTRY

Adopted by the National Catholic Young Adult Ministry Association Board

Who Are Young Adults?

Young adulthood embraces a large, diverse, mobile population which is generally understood as late teens to the mid-thirties. Rather than referring solely to an age group, the term *young adult* more accurately describes a passage, an attitude, an orientation, a life experience. Young adulthood is that stage of life in which directions are sought, choices are tested, and commitments are made. (United States Catholic Conference, *Planning for Single Young Adult Ministry: Directions for Ministerial Outreach* [Washington, D.C.: United States Catholic Conference, 1981], p. 10).

Young adults can be found in all states of life and in every community in our society, from farms to small towns to large cities. They represent diverse educational, vocational, social, political, cultural, and spiritual structures. Whether single or in couples, with or without children, young adults cannot be stereotyped.

Within *early adulthood* three general stages of development are identifiable, each involving different life tasks. The rate at which young adults move through these stages may differ according to their life states and their unique cultures.

The first stage usually occurs in the late teens and early twenties, when developing personal identity, establishing intimate relationships with God and others, and exploring career options are the life tasks. Short-term commitments appeal to younger adults because of the variety of options open to them.

While many young adults are faith-filled, they often do not practice their faith in more traditional ways until they move into the next stage, which usually includes persons in their mid-twenties. At this time, life tasks involve making career moves, eventually establishing themselves in one specific career, and choosing a more permanent life state. Young adults begin to tie into parish life, often by seeking a meaningful experience of worship or a welcoming faith community. They are committed to the search for life's meaning, for truth and for authenticity.

When young adults reach their late twenties and early thirties, they begin to seek a community that both affirms and challenges as they establish roots. They make more permanent commitments, use their previous life experiences to make decisions about the future, make a contribution to their world, and become more involved in parish life. (Department of Education, *Young Adult Ministry Resources,* [Washington, D.C.: United States Catholic Conference, 1988], pp. 35-37).

It is important to realize that there are some young adults whose primary life task is survival.

What Is Ministry with Young Adults?

In defining ministry, we always turn to the life experience of our teacher, Jesus Christ, who ministered through word and example. His preaching was proactive as he taught that the reign of God was near. His action was responsive. Jesus discovered

(Jennell Bergwall)

the needs of people within his society and served accordingly. In responding to them, he enabled them to meet one another's needs.

Young adult ministry is a response to the needs of young adults, an invitation to share their gifts with the larger community, and a challenge to live gospel values in the world. On diocesan, parish, or one-to-one levels, young adult ministers journey alongside young adults, enabling them to take responsibility for their lives of faith, build community within an intergenerational Church, and grow spiritually. The ministers collaborate with young adults to awaken and direct their baptismal call of discipleship. Through resulting social, service, spiritual, or educational ministries, a process is begun empowering young adults to own the ministry. Rather than offering set programs, the process changes and evolves as young adults develop the ministry. The talents and gifts they discover affirm young adults and encourage them to continue the mission of building the kingdom.

Proposed Foundational Principles

1. Young Adult Ministry is rooted in Jesus Christ, who, through his life, death, and resurrection, is the revelation of God among us, constantly made present through the Holy Spirit.

2. Young Adult Ministry is lived out in Christian discipleship, through which a personal relationship with God in Jesus Christ is enhanced and sustained.

3. Young Adult Ministry grows out of the life and mission of the Church, through which the presence and work of Jesus are continued in the world.

4. Young Adult Ministry is situated within the context of lifelong formation which fosters Catholic Christian faith through trust, belief, and action.

5. Young Adult Ministry calls them to a sense of vocation as they bring a Christian presence and dedication to the marketplace or environment where they share their gifts.

6. Young Adult Ministry recognizes the young adult as part of a family system and the family as the first church. Any experience within that system will either facilitate or inhibit a person's growth.

7. Young Adult Ministry recognizes and is sensitive to the differences among young adults in rural, urban, and suburban settings and in various ethnic and racial groups, economic levels, and life situations. It responds to the needs and opportunities each offers to growth in full Christian maturity.

8. Young Adult Ministry values the unique cultural expressions of the faith of young adults and believes that faith enriches the culture and that culture influences faith.

Proposed Operational Principles

1. Because many in our communities are young adults, churches that want to attract young adults welcome them, provide good liturgy and preaching, and involve them in significant and visible ways (e.g. Sunday worship, councils, etc.).

2. Because young adults are unlikely to be visible at Sunday worship, outreach and hospitality are effective hallmarks of this ministry.

3. Because young adulthood is associated with diversity (e.g. in age, culture, and family background), ministries need to respond appropriately through varied services, styles, and schedules.

4. Because young adulthood is a time of testing and forming commitments, ministry opportunities should offer options and flexibility.

5. Because young adulthood is a time in which young adults are making sense of their lives, the Church recognizes the need to gather them to break bread and to tell their stories within relationships of trust. It is here that skilled listeners will discover the needs, visions, and ideals of young adults.

6. Because young adult ministry unfolds within a comprehensive approach, it involves prayer and presence, listening and healing, enablement and integration. (United States Catholic Conference, *Planning for Single Young Adult Ministry: Directions for Ministerial Outreach* [Washington, D.C.: United States Catholic Conference], pp. 18-21).

7. Because young adults often work out of a searching faith style, young adult ministry utilizes adult models of formation and a comfortable place for questions, struggle, doubt, understanding, and acceptance.

8. Because their lives are rooted in relationships, young adults should be ministered to in a relational context and offered models and mentors. Each community is responsible for identifying a qualified and accessible staff person (paid or volunteer) as a contact to meet the needs of young adults and to ensure continuity.

9. Because young adults are sensitive to the media, creativity, and the use of vivid imagery are effective complements to personal invitation.

10. Because young adults spend much of their time in the marketplace of a highly competitive and consumer-oriented society, the Church needs to offer a critique and an alternative value system to assist them in making sound ethical decisions and vocational choices.

11. Because young adults often return to the Church at times of passage or crisis (often through a sacramental context), church leaders need to be sensitive, open to their needs, and welcoming.

12. Because young adults come into contact with the Church through a variety of situations and because ministry is a collaborative work, young adult ministry seeks to organize its actions on a variety of levels (parish, parish cluster, city, diocese, etc.) and share resources with a variety of organizations (RCIA, adult education, campus ministry, etc.)

13. Because many young adults exhibit an interest in bettering the situation of the poor and oppressed and because this work is constitutive of the Gospel, ministry compels them to meet human needs and address the structures and institutions that support injustice.

14. Because young adults live in a religiously diverse society (evidenced by a high number of interfaith marriages), young adult ministry has a corresponding sensitivity.

· · · · ·

Parish Outreach to Young Adults

By Rev. John Cusick, Archdiocese of Chicago
Diane M. Guy, SND, Diocese of Richmond
Margaret O'Brien, OSU, Diocese of Rockville Centre

In preparation for the 1993 international gathering in Denver, parishes have a unique opportunity to be aware of the young adult members of the Catholic community.

Young adults are women and men in their twenties and thirties searching in a particular way for meaning in their lives. Often away from their home of origin, mostly single, sometimes married, engaging the work-world seriously for the first time, and forging an adult identity, young Catholics are looking to the Church whose mission and spiritual dimension they know and understand. During this year of preparation, it is the privilege of members of the Roman Catholic Church to welcome young adults in an intentional way into the worshipping parish community.

This moment is an important juncture in the faith life of the young adult and in the parish life of the faith community. Young adults, because of their previous experience (or lack thereof) in religious education, confirmation preparation, and campus ministry, are choosing to look toward a parish community during this stage of life when their personal focus is on work, identity, and intimacy issues. At this time they are choosing life-styles and pondering vocational goals.

Young adults are vital to the Church of today. Their presence in the Catholic community means that the Body of Christ is renewed by the hope embodied in their energy, questions, and witness. Catholics affiliate with the Church at the same rate today as thirty years ago. However, younger Catholics are more casual both in how they approach the Church and in their active participation in everything from Sunday liturgy to more structured organized programs.

The mode for parish communities to respond to these younger adults is wrapped within traditional Catholic values of hospitality and invitation. The challenge at every level of parish leadership is to be proactive with young adults who are searching for meaning in their lives; it is to invite them to seek that meaning through active participation in the Church.

During this year the people of the parish must reach out and invite young adults to participate. If the community is serious about the faith life of young Catholics, the parishioners will need to tell them so personally and as often as possible. There is no substitute for personal endeavor. Printed announcements in parish bulletins will not suffice.

Programming for young adults can take many forms:

• Young adults can be invited to participate in what is already happening in the current life of the parish; e.g., social ministry, liturgical ministry, catechesis, base communities, parish councils.

• Parish staff can empower young adults to create their own parish peer ministry of welcoming and planning events relevant for persons in their twenties and thirties. These gatherings will offer opportunities to socialize, pray, discuss, and serve the community. Young people have much to offer; we must listen to them!

• Most importantly, parish and campus communities must be more sensitive in caring for young adults when they need the Church. These moments include their weddings, baptisms of their children, funerals of family and friend, confirmation. All of these are key moments of evangelization.

• Parish councils can encourage adult parishioners to reflect on their privileged role as mentor.

This role is so vital - the supporter of life's dream - as young adults shape their vocational goals.

- Given the fact that young adults often seek counsel from parish staffs, these professionals can intentionally program for young adults in areas such as moral decision making, faith in the work place, spirituality.

- Parishes should engender an interest in this international gathering among the young adult community; making available all information coming from the diocesan coordinator and including young adults in all parish plans and programs.

- Parish staffs need to encourage young adults to gather for planning details of the trip.

- Capitalizing on the fact that this gathering in Denver is international, parish leadership can help facilitate gatherings of young adults which celebrate the multicultural heritage of the Roman Catholic Church.

Selected Bibliography

Fowler, James W., *Becoming Adult, Becoming Christian: Adult Development and Christians Faith* (San Francisco: Harper and Row, 1984).

O'Brien Margaret, OSU, *Discovering Your Light: Common Journeys of Young Adults* (New York: Resurrection Press, 1991).

Roof, Wade Clark, with the assistance of Bruce Greer, Mary Johnson, SND, Andrea Leibson, Karen Loeb, Elizabeth Souza, *A Generation of Seekers: Baby Boomers and the Quest for a Spiritual Style* (San Francisco: Harper Collins, March 1993).

Parks, Sharon, *The Critical Years: The Young Adult Search for a Faith to Live By* (San Francisco: Harper Collins, March, 1993).

Young Adult Ministry, Archdiocese of Chicago, *Re-Generating Catholicism* (Chicago: ACTA Publications, 1991), videotape.

Young Adult Ministry, Diocese of Richmond, *How to: Guidelines and Suggestions for Young Adult Ministry* (Richmond, 1990).

· · · · ·

A Dozen Things Any Parish Can Do for Young Adults

By Ron Bagley, CJM
(Reprinted from Principles for Ministry with Young Adults. *Network Paper, No. 44, with permission of Don Bosco Multimedia.)*

Not every parish will be able to organize a comprehensive ministry for young adults. This involves organizing a well-trained team of young adults who will carry out this ministry and providing the necessary resources for the implementation of a wide variety of programs. But any parish that has an interest in young adults and the great gift they are to the Church can do any number of the following:

1. Develop a mailing list of all parishioners who are away at college. Ask the students or their parents to submit their names and college addresses. Before the Christmas break send each of them a Christmas card and an invitation to a party while they are home.

2. The pastor can invite a small group of young adults to have dinner with him at the rectory. This is a good idea in small parishes where the pastor is alone and there are only a few young adults. During dinner they may be invited to talk about their needs and how they can be met in the parish as well as how their gifts can be used in the parish. The pastor may invite a few young adults periodically (e. g., once a month) until he has covered all the young adults of the parish.

3. Those who preach can use examples of single young adults and their lives in their homilies. Too often the illustrations used in homilies relate to those who are married and have children. Take examples from the lives of college students and those who work in the world. This simple inclusion makes a world of difference to the young adult members of the congregation.

4. Make sure that young adults are included among the various liturgical ministries (lectors, Eucharistic ministers, music ministers, ushers, greeters, etc.). It gives a clear message to anyone who enters that young adults are welcome here. Also include young adults on the parish council and all parish committees. Their presence will ensure that the gifts and concerns of young adults are not forgotten by the parish.

5. At Sunday Mass have someone publicly welcome all visitors and new parishioners. Many young adults fall into this category. This is especially true in parishes which offer a Sunday evening Mass. A simple greeting can help them feel welcome. Of course, greeters at the door enhance this sense of hospitality. Perhaps greeters (especially those who are young adults) can be particularly on the look out for young adults visitors.

6. The parish can provide child care during the most heavily attended Masses. Many parents of preschool children are unable to attend Mass together or to participate when they do because of the amount of attention their children demand. No one who advocates a *crying room* has ever spent much time in one. It simply fosters the notion that it is alright to misbehave. Many fine, parish child-care programs are actually doing preschool religious education, so that the child benefits as well.

7. A sponsor-couple approach to marriage preparation enables young adults to minister to their peers. Fine training programs are available for the sponsor couples. A couple preparing for marriage has the opportunity to learn from and reflect with people who know what they are experiencing and how they feel. This is a form of mentoring. Lasting friendships can result from these programs.

8. The parish staff (including the pastor, all associates, the secretary, **everyone!**) needs to have a welcoming attitude toward young adults who are not registered when they approach the parish for services. Many of these young adults are not tied to a particular parish and may not attend church regularly. How are they received when they come to the parish office or call on the phone to ask for a letter of recommendation, to get married, to have a baby baptized, or to arrange for the death of a parent. Make every attempt to be friendly, kind, and hospitable. Look for ways to be helpful and to show understanding of their situation. Since this is one of the few encounters a parish might have with such young adults, make it a positive experience. Make this the topic of discussion at a future staff meeting.

9. Plan occasional social activities for young adults. There are very few opportunities for them to gather with their peers in a wholesome and positive atmosphere. This could be as simple as a volleyball night or happy hour, or may involve more planning like a camping trip or dance. Invite some young adults to be involved in the planning.

10. Offer an overnight retreat. These take many forms and styles and could include any number of topics. Some young adults prefer retreats which focus on discussion and interaction; others want a more quiet and reflective atmosphere. Successful retreats include some of each. Once again, it is good to invite some young adults to be a part of the planning.

11. Sponsor a speaker (or a series) on a topic of interest to young adults. This is a good opportunity to use local resource people. Such topics might include: moral decision making, fundamentalism, sexuality, prayer, relationship, loneliness, women in the Church, etc. The topics from the sessions in this book may warrant further consideration.

12. Provide meaningful service opportunities for young adults. Many young adults are in positions of responsible leadership in the world. Offering them a chance to use their gifts in the Church may help them to feel closer ties. Such opportunities might include working in the parish youth program, volunteering in the parish's outreach to those in need, serving as a sponsor in the RCIA, etc.

Editor's Note: Offer regularly scheduled bible studies and devotions to the Blessed Sacrament. Invite young adults to reflect together and develop a deeper experience of the transcendent in their lives.

. . . . .

TEN THINGS EVERY PARISH CAN DO WITH YOUTH

HOW TO BECOME A YOUTH-FRIENDLY PARISH COMMUNITY

By John Roberto

Center For Youth Ministry Development

The tremendous growth of comprehensive parish youth ministries over the last two decades is one of the great success stories of the Catholic Church in the United States. Many parishes have worked long and hard to create engaging youth programming that both addresses the needs and concerns for youth and promotes their healthy development and growth in faith. By organizing teams of adults and youth to plan and conduct programming, these parishes have watched their efforts multiply - reaching more and more young people.

Other parishes look at this commitment of resources and energy and because of geography or size or social situation, make the judgment that they cannot organize a comprehensive ministry with youth. Frustrated by their inability to organize youth programming, they do little to minister to youth.

The truth is that every parish has the marvelous opportunity to minister to youth. Every parish can create a youth-friendly parish community. Every parish can become a community where young people are valued, where their gifts and talents are recognized and utilized, and where they are acknowledged as full-fledged members of the parish community. Every parish can become a church for youth.

Whether or not a parish has formal youth programming, there are dozens of things every parish can do to become more youth-friendly. Here are ten ideas to start you thinking and acting.

1. *Leadership.* Invite young people into leadership roles in the parish community. This is a great way to build a mentoring relationship between adults and youth and to utilize the gifts and talents of youth in the parish community. Think about all the possibili-

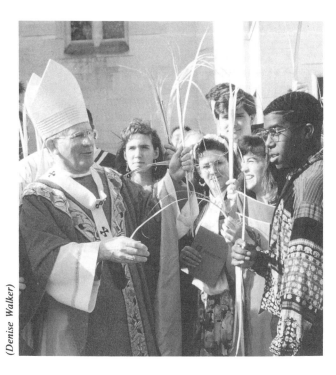

(Denise Walker)

ties for leadership in the ministries, programs, and activities of the parish. Examples: parish council, parish committees (liturgy, social activities, religious education), organizing parish social events, serving as catechists for children.

2. *Sunday Worship and Seasonal Celebrations.* A first strategy is to develop Sunday worship that is youth-sensitive and youth-involving. Examples: prayers for youth concerns at Sunday liturgy; family liturgy involving youth and parents; youth-oriented songs that young people have selected from the hymnal or missalette to be used at Masses they attend; homilies that contain at least one example which will relate directly to the lives of young people. A second strategy is to involve youth in liturgical ministries, such as lectors, greeters (hospitality ministry), and music ministry (voice or instruments).

Identify youth who are good singers or instrumentalists (check out the school band and choir) and get them involved in music ministry. Identify artists and encourage them to use their gifts in planning the environment for the various liturgical seasons. Establish an apprenticeship program and/or specific liturgical and skill training for youth involved in liturgical ministries. A third strategy is to involve youth in the preparation and leadership of seasonal (Advent/Christmas, Lent/Easter, Pentecost) or ethnic celebrations. For example, young people with dramatic and musical talent can take responsibility for a *living* Stations of the Cross during Holy Week.

3. *Youth Worship.* Schedule special youth Eucharistic liturgies, prayer services, or communal reconciliation services periodically so that youth will have contact with the parish. Involve youth in the planning of these services so that the liturgies reflect their preferences in music, prayer styles, storytelling, and environment. Examples: a parish back-to-school liturgy, a liturgy for the Feast of the Holy Family, a graduation liturgy.

4. *Service.* Incorporate a youth component into parish service projects by identifying which parish groups are engaged in service to the community and then working with them to include youth in their present and future service projects. A second idea is to utilize national programs that are already developed, such as Operation Rice Bowl from Catholic Relief Services and invite youth to participate. A third idea is to utilize diocesan or community service projects that are already developed and invite youth to participate as a parish group.

5. *Intergenerational/Family.* Conserve time and energy by organizing intergenerational and/or family programming that includes youth. This type of programming has so many benefits for youth, such as building understanding and harmony across the generations. Explore the possibilities of designing or redesigning existing programming with a family or intergenerational focus. Examples: social, picnics, worship experiences, religious education, parish mission, Advent programming, Lenten programming, and ethnic events and celebrations. A second strategy is to make available specific parent-youth events by utilizing guest speakers, video-based programs, or packaged programs from the diocese or other agencies. Examples: workshops on communication skills, negotiation, and problem-solving skills; programs on topics of common interest to youth and parents (sexuality, moral values, careers, etc.); parent-teen retreat programs.

6. *Retreat.* Offer an annual youth retreat (weekend or overnight) for the youth of the parish. Each annual retreat could have a unique theme, thereby

making each year different. You can use outside resource people to conduct the retreat in the parish or you can bring the parish to an existing retreat program sponsored by your diocese or by the local retreat house.

7. *Newsletter.* Initiate regular communication with the youth of the parish through the use of a monthly or seasonal newsletter. This can be developed as a separate publication, incorporated into an existing parish newsletter or inserted into the Sunday bulletin. A group of youth (with or without parents/adults) from the parish can work as a team writing and preparing the newsletter. The newsletter can contain articles for youth enrichment, such as self-help articles, reflections on youth issues and concerns, scripture reflections, youth prayers, and recommendations for T.V. and movie viewing. A parish can also develop a parent-page of helpful insights and information which can be mailed to each parent with the youth newsletter.

8. *Youth Events.* Develop seasonal youth events to gather the youth of parish. Even if a parish does not have formal youth ministry programming, it can offer occasional events or programs for the youth of the parish. These events build a sense of parish identity among the youth and can be organized as one-time events, such as social activities, athletic activities, relevant cultural experiences, special trips, service projects, and educational programs. They can also be organized as a short series of programs, such as a speaker or video series on topics of interest to young people. You may be able to sponsor youth events by utilizing existing diocesan youth activities or by co-sponsoring a program with other churches or youth organizations in your community.

9. *Guidance.* Develop and distribute a directory of recommended counseling resources that youth and their families can use for assistance in times of trouble. A parish can print cards with phone numbers of crisis intervention services, support groups, resource people, and agencies. The directory can also include a list of community educational programs and resources (books and videos) for youth and/or parents that address adolescent/family concerns and problems.

10. *Community Calendar.* Create a calendar that lists all of the recommended parish and community events for youth and for families in a given month or season (3-4 months). This is a great way to alert youth and their families to upcoming programs, activities, and events and to invite them to participate. Make sure that the calendar includes pertinent information on each event. Mail the calendar to every youth and their parents or insert it into the parish bulletin. Be sure to highlight parish activities.

. . . . .

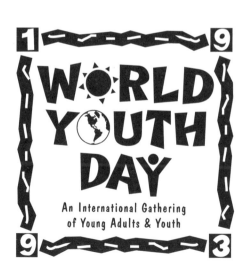

WORLD YOUTH DAY CATECHETICAL MATERIALS

INTRODUCTION

Jesus Is the Real Fullness of Life for Young People

*By Rev. Alfred McBride, O'Praem.
Project Director for Catechetical Materials*

On Palm Sunday 1992, Pope John Paul II announced the VIII World Youth Day 1993. After speaking of the joy of the journey in which young people can encounter Jesus Christ, he said:

> I invite all Christian communities dioceses, associations, movements - to undertake a thorough and profound process of preparation and catechesis for young people and with young people, to be lived as spiritual pilgrimage directed towards the gathering in Denver.

Responding to the pope's request, the bishops of the United States have commissioned catechetical materials to be used with young adults; college students; and youth in parish programs, schools, universities, and families. This is the purpose of the catechetical materials that follow and that are for young people at the various age levels.

These materials implement the theme of the World Youth Day: "I came that they might have life and have it more abundantly" (Jn 10:10). The USCC Department of Education engaged Father Jude Winkler to develop an exegesis of the text. From Father Winkler's reflection, the USCC Department of Education staff drew the following four catechetical themes:

1. Jesus offers us real life.
   God's creative initiative generates all life.
   God extends life and love freely.
   Real, authentic, abundant life is the very life of God.

2. To choose Jesus is to choose life.
   God's life and love draws us to him; we are invited to respond.
   Jesus is the Lord of life; the author and source of life without end.
   The decision for life in Christ is itself God's gift.

3. Life lived in relationship with others is life worth living.
   Each person is created in the image of God.
   We are united to one another in Christ.
   The Church is a sign and instrument of salvation.

4. To live fully is to pour out one's self for others.
   Abundant life is life in the Holy Spirit.
   Jesus pours out his life, his Spirit for us.
   Generous self-giving proclaims Christ.

The department staff members convened ten catechetical experts from around the United States to plan catechetical materials for VIII World Youth Day. The consultants represented leadership of the various age levels of youth and their multicultural backgrounds.

Their discussions resulted in identifying a number of objectives for each of the themes and suggesting a list of writers for the materials. The selected writers were asked to produce materials for two lessons/sessions and one retreat day. The commendable and positive results of their efforts are offered to you as a catechetical resource in preparation for VII World Youth Day.

WORLD YOUTH DAY
AN INTERNATIONAL GATHERING OF YOUNG ADULTS & YOUTH

(Gary Allen Brown)

Please consider these materials as auxiliary resources to your regular religious education programs. Use them in any sequence that suits your needs. Do not feel constrained to connect them with any special liturgical feast or season. Link them to the plans you have already set in place. Treat them as stimulants to your own creativity and adapt them to your personal situation.

The purpose of this year of preparation for World Youth Day is to open the hearts of all our young people to the saving power of Jesus Christ. This is a time for evangelizing our young people, calling them to respond to the grace of Jesus by a new, living, and active faith. In turn they should become evangelizers for Christ, sharing their faith in him with others and inviting them to a deeper union with him and the Church, the effective sign and sacrament of salvation in the world.

For Hispanics

A Spanish translation of the materials is available upon request. The writers have addressed multicultural needs through a process-oriented approach and in the provision of suggested resources in these areas.

The Song

Take a look at the special World Youth Day song which has been commissioned for this occasion. We believe your young people will find its spirited words and music very appealing. The song will serve as a spiritual and emotional binding force for youth from all over the world.

Many Cultures, One Church

Remember that this is a celebration of faith by youth from all over the world. It is more than an American gathering. The Church of the United States is the host for the assembly. The event will be a symbol of the worldwide communion of the Church. The unique multicultural mix of American Catholic ethnic groups from all continents is a microcosm of the universal communion of the Church. Beyond the many differences is the unity expressed by identification with the communion of the Church. Young Catholics from every corner of the planet will convene in Denver to affirm the solidarity of their faith in Jesus Christ.

The Pilgrim Model

The context for the World Youth Day is the sign of the pilgrim. Thousands of youth will journey thousands of miles to the mountains of Denver to deepen their encounter with Jesus. At the head of this pilgrimage will be the Youth Cross. First handed by the Holy Father to young people in Rome in 1984, this Youth Cross has led subsequent pilgrimages to a second Rome pilgrimage and to Buenos Aires, Santiago de Compostella, and Czestochowa.

The connection of the Youth Cross and the pilgrimage illustrates Christ's call to discipleship. It points to the interior faith journey of youth who make the pilgrimage. It dramatizes the challenge to bring Christ's life, love, justice, and mercy to the world. The materials provided here are designed to awaken and enhance this modern day pilgrimage.

Importance of Preparation

A spiritual event is effective in proportion to the faith preparation that precedes it. Our Blessed Mother and the 120 disciples spent nine days in prayer before receiving the Holy Spirit at Pentecost. A prayerful catechesis will lead our youthful pilgrims to the *Lord's Mountain* in Denver. The more profound their faith preparation, the more their hearts will be opened to the "abundant life" of Jesus Christ on that day of grace.

Life Abundant

Of course the pilgrimage will not end at Denver. The journey's ultimate goal is eternal life in heaven. Our Holy Father has chosen a life theme for those among us in whom vitality is most evident. One of the wonders we can ponder is that the ones who hunger most for even more life are those who are seemingly most full of it. The yearning of youth to live life more fully is a gift of God. Our suggested catechetical materials build upon this truth and offer you ways to help young people become more conscious of Jesus as the real response to youth's hunger for authentic living. Pope John Paul II teaches the real meaning of this life from Christ in his World Youth Day message for 1993.

At the climax of revelation, the Incarnate Word proclaims, "I am the life." (Jn 14:6), and, "I came so that they might have life" (Jn 10:10). But what life? Jesus' intention was clear: the very life of God, which surpasses all the possible aspirations of the human heart (cf. 1 Cor 2:9). The fact is that through the grace of Baptism we are already God's children. (cf. 1 Jn 3:1-2).

Psalms of Pilgrimage

In the Hebrew scriptures, King David provided words and music for his people on pilgrimage. Psalms 121-125 offer us a rich biblical resource for praying with the world's young people. By a happy coincidence with Denver, the first of these psalms pictures pilgrims arriving at the mountains. "I lift up my eyes to the mountains. Whence shall help come to me? The Lord is your guardian" (Ps 121:1,5).

Let these inspiring words guide you and your young people in this year of faith pilgrimage. May the whole experience awaken in all of us the needs of the troubled, the poor, the vulnerable, and those in most need of care. May the road to Denver be a road beyond to fuller faith and life and to the eternal for the young and for all of us.

Director's Note: I wish to thank Dr. Carole Eipers, Rev. James DiGiacomo, SJ, and Mr. Donald McCrabb for their prompt, professional, and faith-filled response to the call to prepare these materials. I also appreciate the wise guidance received from Sister Elaine McCarron, SCN, and Rev. John Pollard.

Suggested Resources for Catechetical Guidance on Multicultural Sensitivity

National Conference of Catholic Bishops, *The Hispanic Presence: Challenge and Commitment,* A Pastoral Letter on Hispanic Ministry, English/Spanish text (Washington, D.C.: United States Catholic Conference, 1983), Pub. No. 891-6.

National Conference of Catholic Bishops, *National Pastoral Plan for Hispanic Ministry* (the U.S. bishop's challenge to Catholics to focus on and address the pastoral needs of the nation's Hispanic Catholics), English/Spanish text (Washington, D.C.: United States Catholic Conference, 1987), Pub. No.199-7.

African American bishops, *What We Have Seen and Heard,* A Pastoral Letter on Evangelization, 1983.

NCCB Secretariats for the Liturgy and for Black Catholics, *Plenty Good Room: The Spirit and Truth of African American Catholic Worship* (furthers the call for the installation of a distinctly African American flavor to the Roman Catholic celebration), (Washington, D.C.: United States Catholic Conference, 1991), Pub. No. 385-X.

National Conference of Catholic Bishops, *A Time For Remembering, Reconciling and Recommitting Ourselves as a People: A Pastoral Reflection on the V Centenary and Native American Peoples* (Washington, D.C.: United States Catholic Conference, 1992), Pub. No. 470-8.

National Catholic Educational Association, *The People: Reflections of Native Peoples on the*

Catholic Experience in North America, (Washington, D.C.: NCEA, 1992), See especially chapter VII, Practical Helps for Teachers.

National Catholic Educational Association, *A Catholic Response to the Asian Presence,* Catechetical materials are listed for: Chinese, Indian, Japanese, Korean, Philippine, Vietnamese, Cambodian, Hmong, and Laotian ethnic groups Washington, D.C.: NCEA, 1991).

. . . . .

JUNIOR HIGH
LESSON 1

The Kingdom through Kinship
By Carole M. Eipers, D. Min.
Director of Religious Education
Archdiocese of Chicago

Catechetical Plan
for Junior High Youth

Jesus came to provide the ultimate answer to the yearning for life and for the infinite which his heavenly Father had poured into our hearts when he created us.

Pope John Paul II
World Youth Day Address 1993

Scriptural Focus: "I came so that they might have life and have it more abundantly" (Jn 10:10).
Catechetical Theme: Life lived in good relationship with self, others, our world, and God is "abundant life."

Movements

1. To explore what it means to be in good relationship with self, others, creation, and God.

2. To define rights and responsibilities in the context of our various relationships.

3. To examine the ways in which we can nurture good relationships.

4. To explore the work of the Holy Spirit in human relationships.

Catechetical Lesson

A. Sharing Experience

1. A common expression we hear is "They have such a good relationship!" This expression may be used to describe friends, family members, teammates, co-workers, etc. What do we mean by a "good relationship"?

2. The junior high people could work alone, with a partner, or in small groups. Each division will take one of the following relationships to explore: relationship with self, relationship with other people, relationship with creation, relationship with God.

3. After a topic has been chosen by the groups, allow time for the groups to reflect on a person they know who has a good relationship in their topic area. They could jot down their thoughts about the person's good relationship, e.g. adjectives that describe it, examples that illustrate how the relationship is "good."

4. If the participants are working with partners or a small group, have them share their stories of the person's good relationship. Have them prepare a summary that describes the particular "good relationship" which is their topic. If individuals have worked alone, they would share their reflection with the whole group.

5. Have the whole group review the summaries. Are there other words or phrases which they would add to any of the four relationships?

B. Relating Scripture and Tradition

In addition to our knowledge and experiences of good relationships, the Scripture and Tradition offer insights into what good relationships with self, others, creation, and God are like.

Scripture

Assign individuals, partners, or groups to read the following scripture passages and answer these questions:

Which kind of good relationships does this passage talk about? What are we told about the qualities of this type of a good relationship?

Relationship with self:
"Let your yes mean yes. . . ." Mt 5:33-37
"Are not you more important than [the birds in the sky]?" Mt 6:26-33
A good tree produces good fruit. Lk 6:43-49

Relationship with others:
". . . [L]ove one another. . . ." Jn 15:12-13

". . . salt of earth. . . light of world" Mt 5:13-16
Whoever wants to be first must serve. Mk 10:35-45
". . .[L]ove your enemies. . . ." Lk 6:27-38

Relationship with creation:
The reign of God is like sowing good seed. Mt 13:24-30
Even the sea obeys him. Lk 8:22-25
". . .[H]e was passing through a field of grain. . . ." Mk 2:23-28

Relationship with God:
Vine and branches. Jn 15:1-8
You are my friends. Jn 15:14-15
". . .[A]sk and you will receive. . . ." Lk 11:5-13

Tradition

Tradition of the past and our living Tradition as a Catholic community of faith offers us wisdom about good relationships.

Each of the seven sacraments has relational implications. Take each of the sacraments and discuss what it says about our relationship with self, others, creation, and God.

Catholic/ethnic/cultural groups have religious traditions/ceremonies/rituals which express wisdom regarding relationships. Have students share their own experiences and/or invite individuals of other cultures to come and share their traditions.

After these experiences, summarize together what our Catholic tradition and ethnic cultural practices say about good relationships.

C. Impacting Contemporary Life

We have explored what good relationships are through looking at our own experiences and at the wisdom of the Scriptures and Tradition. How can these insights be applied to our society today and to our own lives?

1. Have the participants review the insights they have noted regarding each of the relationships: with self, others, creation, God. Are there any other words, phrases which they would add?

2. Of these four relationships, have each student name the relationships which they believe is most crucial for our world today and which need the most work to become a "good relationship."

3. Have small groups discuss and report to the whole group on:
   • The signs that this particular relationships is not good or is in danger of becoming not good;
   • The relationship;
   • What it takes to make this relationship good or at least better.

4. After the reports, have the whole group choose one specific action they will take to improve one area of relationship.

D. Praying

The abundant life that Jesus gives us is the very life of God. It is a life of infinite love and forgiveness. We receive that life through our baptism, our participation in the Eucharist, and other sacraments. We regain it in the sacrament of reconciliation. Our life of prayer and practical love opens us continually to divine life. Our connection with Jesus is as intimate as a branch with a vine. Jesus says. "I am the vine, you are the branches. Whoever remains in me and I in him will bear much fruit, because without me you can do nothing" (Jn 15:5).

Jesus calls us to an "abundant life" which is found in and expressed through good loving relationships with self, others, creation, God. This prayer time is an opportunity to focus on our individual need for good relationships and the areas in which we need God's help to grow in order to make our relationships better.

1. Begin by gathering in a quiet, comfortable place: the church, a prayer room, outdoors, etc. If possible, appropriate music (taped or live) could accompany the participants' entrance into the prayer space.

2. Prayer Experience:

   Opening: Sign of the Cross

   Scripture Reading: Choose one from Part B.

   Sung Response: World Youth Day Song or appropriate psalm

   Reflection Focus: How does Jesus call me to a more abundant life through good relationships? Allow sufficient quiet time for participants to pray quietly.

   Petitions: Jesus offers us abundant life. He invites us into good relationships with ourselves, with other people, with creation, and with himself, the Father, and the Spirit. We can be sure that Jesus will give us the help we need to make our relationships better. Let us ask him for the help we need.

   Ritual Gesture: We have shared peace with one another during this time in our discussion, listening, and prayer. Go now and share a sign of peace with someone beyond our group.

Suggested Uses

Classroom/religious education setting: If the class is very small, choose just one of the relationships as a focus for section C and develop it together.

Extended lesson: In section A, invite people who have "good relationships" in each category to speak with the junior high people.

Have participants interview a person in "good relationship" and report to the class.

Have each group write an article for the parish bulletin/school newsletter/community newspaper suggesting ways in which to make "good relationships" for each category.

In section B, have each group take one sacrament and examine the actual rite/prayers to find what it says about relationships.

Resources

Hna. Maria de la Cruz Aymes, Rdo. Francis J. Buckley, SJ, *Los Sacramentos,* books and videos (Tabor Publishing, 1990).

Huebsch, Bill, *Rethinking Sacraments* (Mystic, Conn.: Twenty-Third Publications, 1989).

Bausch, William, *A New Look at the Sacraments* (Mystic, Conn.: Twenty-Third Publications, 1990).

Crichton, J.D., *Christian Celebration of the Sacraments* (Cassell and Collier Macmillan Publisher, Ltd., 1973).

Cooke, Bernard, *Sacraments and Sacramentality* (Mystic, Conn.: Twenty-Third Publications, 1983).

. . . . .

JUNIOR HIGH
LESSON 2

Gifts with a Lifetime Guarantee

By Carole M. Eipers, D. Min.
Director of Religious Education
Archdiocese of Chicago

Catechetical Plan
for Junior High Youth

Jesus came to meet men and women, to heal the sick and the suffering, to free those possessed by devils and to raise the dead: he gave himself on the Cross and rose again from the dead, revealing that he is the Lord of life: the author and source of Life without end.

Pope John Paul II
World Youth Day Address 1993

Scripture Focus: "I came so that they might have life and have it more abundantly" (Jn 10:10).
Catechetical Theme: To live the "abundant life" which Jesus promises is to give of one's self for others.

Movements

1. To explore models, past and present, of healthy Christian self-giving.

2. To name our individual and communal gifts and the ways in which those gifts can make a difference in our families, schools, parishes, neighborhoods, etc.

3. To experience and identify the sources of nourishment for our living and giving as Christians.

Catechetical Lesson

A. *Sharing Experience*

1. Choose one of the following options.
Use one of several models of healthy Christian self-giving from the past. These might be stories of canonical saints or more recent saintly people. Choose ones who represent a variety of cultures and/or a culture which should have attention in your particular locale.

Show a video which represents an example of healthy self-giving.

Have participants research their favorite saint or saintly person from the past. They can tell the story or dramatize an event from the person's life that illustrates giving of one's self for others.

(Paul Henderson)

2. Allow time for participants to reflect on times when they have given of themselves to others. Ask them to share with a friend one experience of self-giving. What did they give? How? To whom? What was the effect of their gift on themselves and on the other person/persons.

3. Have partners report on or re-enact their examples of Christian self-giving.

4. Have partners work together again to name a "living saint" - someone they know who is a model of healthy Christian self-giving.

5. Have partners design certificates or write letters to the people they have named affirming their self-giving and encouraging and supporting their efforts. Arrange for personal delivery or delivery by mail.

B. *Relating Scripture and Tradition*

Our Scripture and Catholic Tradition challenge us to give of ourselves - our time, talent, and treasure. St. Paul devotes all of chapter 12 in Romans to our duties as Christians. His opening sentence sets the spiritual tone for self-giving. "I urge you therefore, brothers, by the mercies of God, to offer your bodies as a living sacrifice, holy and pleasing to God, your spiritual worship" (Rom 12:1). We are challenged as disciples of Jesus to build up the Church, our community of faith, and to serve others that through us the Holy Spirit may transform the world into the reign of God.

Our Scripture and Tradition also comfort us with the knowledge of God's love and forgiveness, God's desire for our happiness, Jesus' promise of the graces of abundant life, now and eternally, for his followers. The challenge of faith without any comfort would be too much for us. The comfort of our faith without challenge would be empty.

Activities

1. Have participants (individually or in groups) do a scripture search in one of the four Gospels to answer the question: What does Jesus teach us about the giving of ourselves to others? (They may use sayings of Jesus or examples from his actions.)

2. Summarize what Jesus teaches us and the insights gained from the people identified in part A. List what we have learned on newsprint, chalkboard, etc. so that a complete list is visible to the participants.

3. Discuss: Is it easy or difficult to be a self-giving person in today's society? Invite students to respond. They may wish to share stories of their own experiences. When was their self-giving mocked or criticized? Was their giving praised? Did the difference it made in someone's life encouraged them?

4. Have participants do a scripture search in Exodus chapters 3 and 4 and Psalms 121-125 to find the words and stories that strengthen them to give of themselves. Share these with the whole group.

5. Discuss: Besides the words and examples in Scripture, what other sources of encouragement can we use to help us be givers?

6. Allow quiet time for participants to reflect on these sources of encouragement. Ask them to choose the one they will pursue and to share their choice if they wish.

C. Impacting Contemporary Life

The participants will actually engage in self-giving for this part of the plan. Choose from one of the following options.

Brainstorm needs in your parish/school/community. Recognizing the particular gifts of these participants which need could you serve best? Do it together.

Participate together in a planned event in your parish/community, e.g. parish blood drive, community beautification project, AIDS work, etc.

Invite parish/community leaders to come and to share their work with the group. Ask the guests to address one specific way in which the junior high people can contribute to their efforts. Have participants choose which contribution they will make.

Have participants reflect quietly on the needs in their own families. Ask them to focus on one specific way in which they can give of themselves to serve this need. Have them choose a "support partner" who will provide special encouragement through prayers, notes, phone calls, assistance, etc.

D. Praying

Call to Prayer: The God who cares for us and who calls us to give of ourselves in service to others loves to hear the stories of what we have done. Let's tell God the stories of our service.

Sharing: Participants (including adult catechists, etc.) share the stories of their service. Leader affirms each story and each storyteller.

Reflection: Quiet listening to appropriate background music.

Petitions: The God who cares for us and who loves our stories of service is anxious to know our needs. What do you need from God in order to continue giving?

Ritual Gesture: It is not always easy to give of self, let us offer one another some word or sign of encouragement.

Scripture: Matthew 28:16-20

Closing Song: World Youth Day Song

Suggested Uses

Classroom/religious education class: This plan is particularly appropriate for confirmation preparation. Self-giving in service is a way of life for the Christian not a requirement for a sacrament. If students are already confirmed, this lesson provides a reminder of the role of service in the commitment they made.

Extended lesson: In section A, invite the living saints to share a meal with the group or go in pilgrimage to deliver their certificates in person. In section B, have participants interview a person who gives of self and makes a difference in his/her family, school, parish, neighborhood, etc. What encourages that person to continue giving?

Resources

Romero, John Dugan, on Vidmark.

Sr. Thea: Her Own Story: a visual autobiography of a unique African American religious. USCC Office for Publishing and Promotion Services, Video No. 491-0, 50 minutes, $29.95. Call 1-800-235-8722 to order.

The Gift of Katharine Drexel: the life of the foundress of the Sisters of the Blessed Sacrament; highlights her ministry to African Americans and Native Americans. Bureau of Catholic Indian Missions, 2021 H Street N.W., Washington, D.C. 20006. Offering: $20.00. Also available for purchases or rent from: Franciscan Communications, 1229 S. Santee St., Los Angeles, California 90015. Call 1-800-421-8510 to order.

A Time for Miracles: The Life of Elizabeth Ann Seton, First American-born Saint. This program appeared on network television and the video is available in many video rental stores.

Kateri Tekawitha: a book on the life of the first Native-American to be beatified; by F.X. Weiser, SJ; Kateri Center, Caughnawaga, P.Q. Canada.

Mother Teresa: an account of the life and work of a remarkable woman of our time whose dedication to the poor and love of God are an inspiration to all. Videotape, Petrie Productions. Available from: Red Rose Gallery, $19.95. Call 1-800-451-5683 to order.

• • • • •

SENIOR HIGH
LESSON 1

Love Is More Than a Warm Feeling It Is Real Caring

By Rev. James DiGiacomo, SJ
High School Religion Teacher
Region High School, New York, New York

Jesus came to provide the ultimate answer to the yearning for life and for the infinite which his heavenly Father had poured into our hearts when he created us.

Pope John Paul II
World Youth Day Address 1993

(Paul Henderson)

Scriptural Focus: "I came so that they might have life and have it more abundantly" (Jn 10:10).
Catechetical Theme: To live fully is to pour one's self out for others.

Catechetical Plan for Senior High Age Group

A. *Sharing Experience*

Frank Serpico was a New York City detective in the 1970s. At great risk to himself, he not only refused to participate in widespread graft and corruption, but also brought those abuses to light and helped bring about wide-ranging reforms. Al Pacino played Serpico in the movie of the same name. A class of high school juniors was asked, "What made him different from his fellow policemen?" One

student wrote: "When Serpico first entered the police academy, he was the only cadet there who had any humanistic motives for wanting to become a cop. All the other cadets were looking at the job from an economic perspective: good pay, good benefits, and a good pension. They thought nothing about helping their fellow man, even though it should have been their main reason for taking the job."

a. What stories can you share about people who have used their professional jobs to help other people?

b. What is the connection between helping others and really living?

B. *Relating Scripture to Your Life*
(Catechist/Leader Input)

To Live Fully Is to Pour One's Self Out for Others

At the Last Supper, when Jesus had only a few hours left before he would suffer, he found his friends arguing among themselves about who would outrank whom. So he stunned them by taking on the role of the lowliest servant and washing their feet. ". . .Do you realize what I have done for you? You call me 'teacher' and 'master,' and rightly so, for indeed I am. If I, therefore, the master and teacher, have washed your feet, you ought to wash one another's feet. I have given you a model to follow, so that as I have done for you, you should also." (Jn 13:12-15).

If Jesus' closest followers found it hard to grasp what he was about, it shouldn't surprise us if we too sometimes fail to understand. Ask many young or not-so-young persons what it means to be a Christian, and they'll say it means "being nice and not hurting anybody." Nice try, but no cigar. Some come closer when they say it means to love your neighbor. Right. But what is love, and who is my neighbor?

Who Is My Neighbor?

There are numerous persons and groups all around us who need someone to care, who can be served by teenagers in meaningful ways.

The *family* constitutes the group of the nearest "thous" in need.

Here are some ways you can help: "Help set the table for dinner. Volunteer to cook one meal a week. Clean up the kitchen after mealtime. Pick up your things around the house and put them away. Keep your own room or space clean and orderly. Offer to babysit a younger brother or sister. Read to an elderly relative. Keep the noise level down when others are around. Take the dog for a walk."

(*Growing Up Caring*, Bolin, F., Glencoe/McGraw-Hill, 1990, p. 441)

The school becomes a better place when students clean up after themselves in the lunchroom, help slower classmates with difficult lessons, contribute to school-sponsored drives for the needy, and participate in service outreach programs.

The parish and neighborhood can use help in many ways. Check out the church bulletin, the bulletin board in the library and other places, and listen to public service announcements on local radio and television.

a. Can you think of other ways to be a giver as well as a taker?

b. If you have been part of a service program or have had some other experience of serving others, share it with this group.

c. How has this affected you personally?

C. Impacting Contemporary Life
(Catechist/Leader Input)
Serving as a Living

Once we begin to take seriously the notion of following Christ in the service of our neighbor, it can take us very far indeed. Some have made it more than a sideline, more than an extra, and have decided to make their living that way. Patrick Horvath, a graduate of Princeton and Harvard Law School, felt called to work for runaway and abused teenagers at Covenant House in New York. He now works for the Legal Action Center for the Homeless. He told a high school graduating class, "I learned to listen to God's voice within me and I heard it tell me of my desire to devote my life to the poor, not because I should or because I must in order to be holy or just or pious, but because in that devotion I would find God's joy and God's peace."

Like Serpico, Horvath, and many other lay persons, religious sisters, brothers, and priests make the service of God's people their life's work. Not everyone is called this way, but every young Christian can and ought to consider, in choosing a career, how it will affect other people. How much money one can make in a job is very important, but it should not be the only consideration.

a. Discuss some of the major professions and jobs ahead of you.

b. What could be their impact on others?

c. Do they make a difference for good or ill?

d. How would this be important to you in choosing your life's work?

e. In what sense can a career be a vocation?

Resource

The two following films, available in videocassette, are excellent vehicles for dramatizing and inculcating this lesson. Both films are available from Paulist Productions, 17575 Pacific Coast Highway, Pacific Palisades, CA 90272. Price of each: $29.95. Call 1-800-624-8613 to order.

Packy
Packy Rowe, played by Jack Klugman, is an aggressive and abrasive theatrical agent who has a very low opinion of himself. When he dies and goes to meet God, he takes his flamboyant exterior with him. As he gets to know God, played by Bob Newhart, he discovers that God's values are not quite his own. He is surprised to discover that God was a lot happier with him than he was with himself. The reason for this: Packy's repeated acts of kindness toward other people. His life has been a success, he learns, because he has loved much. God and Packy enter eternity together.

A Slight Change in Plans
In South America on a business trip, John Hopkins joins a team of priests working in a Lima barrio and experiences God as he never has before. Returning to the United States, John's new values bring him into direct conflict with his businessman father and with the company for which he works. He sees firsthand the spiritual hunger of many of his associates: a classmate has committed suicide, a friend has joined a cult, and still another has gotten caught up in the pursuit of things. He feels called by God to help these people and to bring meaning and joy to their lives. He begins to consider the priesthood, but how does he work that through with his parents and with the girl he intends to marry? Although the second half of the film focuses on the ordained priesthood, the larger issue is the worth of a life lived for others.

Role Play
Mr. and Mrs. Zebedee are interviewed by Phil Donahue or Oprah Winfrey. Why have their sons, James and John, given up a promising career in the fishing business and become itinerant preachers?

For Discussion
Do you know any students at school who are givers rather than takers? How can you tell? Why do you think they are that way?

Besides money and security, what would you look for in a prospective career?

Prayer
Lord, sometimes I feel as if I'm two different people. One wants to be generous, to reach out to

others, to add to the goodness in the world. The other just wants to look out for Number One. Help me to get out of myself and to be a person for others like Jesus Christ, our Lord. Amen.

Additional Resources

Sr. Thea: Her Own Story: a visual autobiography of a unique African American religious. USCC Office for Publishing and Promotion Services, Video No. 491-0, 50 minutes, $29.95. Call 1-800-235-8722 to order.

The Gift of Katharine Drexel: the life of the foundress of the Sisters of the Blessed Sacrament; highlights her ministry to African Americans and Native Americans. Bureau of Catholic Indian Missions, 2021 H Street N.W., Washington, D.C. 20006. Offering: $20.00. Also available for purchases or rent from: Franciscan Communications, 1229 S. Santee St., Los Angeles, California 90015. Call 1-800-421-8510 to order.

A Time for Miracles: The Life of Elizabeth Ann Seton, First American-born Saint. This program appeared on network television and the video is available in many video rental stores.

Kateri Tekawitha: a book on the life of the first Native-American to be beatified; by F.X. Weiser, SJ; Kateri Center, Caughnawaga, P.Q. Canada.

Mother Teresa: an account of the life and work of a remarkable woman of our time whose dedication to the poor and love of God are an inspiration to all. Videotape, Petrie Productions. Available from: Red Rose Gallery, $19.95. Call 1-800-451-5683 to order.

· · · · ·

SENIOR HIGH
LESSON 2

If You Want to Be Really Alive, Choose Jesus

By Rev. James DiGiacomo, SJ
High School Religion Teacher
Region High School, New York, New York

> Jesus came to meet men and women, to heal the sick and the suffering, to free those possessed by devils and to raise the dead: he gave himself on the Cross and rose again from the dead, revealing that he is the Lord of life: the author and source of

Life without end.

Pope John Paul II
World Youth Day Address 1993

Scriptural Focus: "I came so that they might have life and have it more abundantly" (Jn 10:10).
Catechetical Theme: To choose Jesus is to choose life.

Catechetical Plan for Senior High Age Group

A. Sharing Experience

The day before his assassination, Dr. Martin Luther King, Jr., spoke to a Memphis gathering about the threats on his life.

> It really doesn't matter with me now. . . . Like anybody, I would like to live a long life. Longevity has its place. But I'm not concerned about that now. I just want to do God's will.

a. Most of you have 50 to 60 years of life ahead of you. What will make life worth living for you?

b. How would you identify with Dr. King's remark that a long life has its place, but doing God's will is the important issue. How would you do God's will?

B. Relating Scripture to Your Life
(Catechist/Leader Input)
No Pain, No Gain

The Synoptic Gospel writers tell us that three separate times on his last journey to Jerusalem, Jesus told his closest followers that he was on his way to suffering and death at the hands of his enemies and that after dying he would rise again. (Mt 16:21, 17:22, 20:17).

The first time, Peter remonstrated him and was severely rebuked. Jesus called him a devil for trying to deflect him from his purpose. Then he made it clear to him and to us: "Whoever wishes to come after me must deny himself, take up his cross, and follow me" (Mt 16:24). Each time after that, when he spelled out the coming events in the clearest language, they were unable to deal with it. Luke says: "But they understood nothing of this; the word remained hidden from them and they failed to comprehend what he said.said" (Lk 18:34).

We may be tempted to feel somewhat superior to the apostles because we know how things turned out and we understand that Jesus had to die for our sins and rise for our salvation (Rom 4:25). But do we, really?

Are you willing to carry a cross?

Do you secretly hope to work a deal whereby you may follow Christ without suffering?

What did Jesus mean when he said, "For whoever wishes to save his life will loose it, but whoever looses his life for my sake will find it" (Mt 16:25)?

C. Impacting Contemporary Life
(Catechist/Leader Input)
Two Kinds of Suffering

Two different kinds of suffering come our way: inevitable and avoidable. Some crosses like sickness, death, and failure, despite our best efforts, can only be accepted and endured. Christians, no less than others, feel the pain, but with a difference.

They know that they are never alone, that Jesus cares and shares the pain with them. To the disciple of Christ, no failure is final, no loss irretrievable. "If God is for us, who can be against us?... What will separate us from the love of Christ? Will anguish, or distress, or persecution, or famine, or nakedness, or peril, or sword?... No, in all these things we conquer overwhelmingly through him who loved us" (Rom 8:31, 35, 37).

We all shrink from pain. Jesus himself, in the garden of Gethsemane, asked to be spared. It's alright to feel this way; we wouldn't be human if we didn't. It's what we do about it that counts. Jesus left the garden and did what he knew he had to do; he took up his cross. Can we be expected to do the same?

There are many people in our society who answer that question with a resounding no. The Christian idea that suffering can be redemptive is more difficult than ever to grasp in a culture that tells us we owe it to ourselves to experience whatever we desire. Ideals like sacrifice, self-denial, and postponement of gratification are met with incomprehension and rejection. A Catholic high school student read an article that said that distributing condoms to teens was a bad idea because it seemed to tell them "When in doubt, go ahead." He wrote, in reply: "This philosophy has made America what it is. As a famous American once said. 'No guts, no glory.' Protection of our inalienable right to pursue happiness has made this country great."

Is our country going to be great by advocating and facilitating immoral behavior?

Some suffering is avoidable and presents us with a choice. Being honest and refusing to cheat can cost us, but that is the price of integrity. Studying instead of partying makes demands. Being sexually responsible and refusing to take risks with our lives and the lives of others can sometimes be very hard to do.

Resisting peer pressure takes a toll; sometimes it really hurts to say no to our friends, even when we know we should. At such times, the choice is between avoiding suffering and being true to ourselves and our sense of right and wrong. Remember that he who loses his life will save it.

Joseph Schultz, a soldier in the German army, made the ultimate choice between life and death on a July day in 1941 outside a village in Yugoslavia. A member of a firing squad ordered to kill a group of peasants, the young soldier refused to participate. He was promptly lined up with the villagers and executed by his comrades. He went to the cross as a martyr of conscience. This inspiring incident is superbly portrayed in a 12-minute film, Joseph Schultz (See Resources.) and is highly recommended as part of this lesson.

a. Some say we have a right not to suffer. What do you think?

b. What do you do about inevitable pain? Avoidable pain?

Through Death to Life

When Jesus foretold his coming death and resurrection, the apostles understandably did not want to listen. The prospect of his suffering was so troubling that they didn't even hear the last part about the resurrection. On the road to Emmaus on Easter Sunday, the risen Jesus still had to say to the two disciples, "Oh, how foolish you are! How slow of of heart to believe all that the prophets spoke! Was it not necessary that the Messiah should suffer these things and enter into his glory" (Lk 24:25-26)?

Without Good Friday, there could be no Easter. This is true not only of Jesus; it is a law of life that shows up in countless ways. Athletes endure pain and exhaustion during training camps, knowing that superior conditioning may make the difference between victory and defeat months later in the title game. Olympic athletes persevere through years of demanding practice and preparation. "No pain, no gain" is a cliche among sports champions. Most of us know, from our own experience, that the most satisfying accomplishments are the ones that cost us the most. Jesus himself points to the example of childbirth: "When a woman is in labor, she is in anguish because her hour has arrived; but when she has given birth to a child, she no longer remembers the pain because of her joy that a child has been born into the world" (Jn 16:21).

Telling the Whole Story

People outside of or on the fringes of Christianity think of it as a grim, joyless way of life that deprives its adherents of the pleasures which are their due. This is also true of many young people who have grown up in the Church but perceive their religious affiliation as a deprivation rather than an enrichment. There are no easy solutions to this pastoral problem, but there are some helpful things that can be done.

One is to speak with them about an aspect of life that is often ignored in religious discourse between the generations. Despite their energy, resiliency, and optimism, many young people are seriously hurting. They have to deal with dysfunctional and broken families, financial insecurity, disappointments and failures, and temptations and pitfalls beyond their years. To deal with the inevitable sufferings, they need comfort and hope. To deal with the avoidable sufferings, they need to be challenged. They need not only Jesus the friend and consoler, but Jesus the man who calls to decision, who is unwavering in his determination to tell it like it is, no matter what the cost. If this uncompromising honesty leaves him with few or even no disciples, then so be it. He is organizing a trip through a narrow gate, and crowds need not apply. If the rich young man cannot stand the idea of not being rich, let him stay home and count his money. If the young fishermen aren't ready to leave their nets, they're not ready to follow him. If Peter doesn't want to hear about the Cross, he can stay in Caesarea Philippi where it's safe, but the first team is going to Jerusalem.

Role Play

Mike Wallace interviews Pontius Pilate on 60 Minutes. Some questions for the Roman governor: Why did he make the decision that he did? How does he respond to some who say the verdict was unjust? What were his impressions of Jesus?

For Discussion

Have you ever postponed gratification/or endured some pain or suffering for an important goal and later been glad that you did? What was it about?

Have you ever resented someone who pushed you very hard and/made great demands, and later been grateful to them? What was it about?

Do you think that being a Christian gets in the way of the pursuit of happiness?

Prayer

Lord, they say that when the going gets tough, the tough get going. That's easy to say, but sometimes we're afraid to take the heat. Help us to have the courage of our convictions and to do your will even when it costs, after the example of Jesus Christ, your Son and our Brother. Amen.

Resources

Joseph Schultz. Videocassette available from Altschul Group, 1560 Sherman Ave., Suite 100,

Evanston, Ill. 60201. Purchase price: $95.00; rental: $60.00. Call 1-800-323-9084 to order.

DiGiacomo, J., "Telling the Jesus Story," *Today's Catholic Teacher,* (Nov.-Dec. 1981), p. 22.

Sr. Thea: Her Own Story: a visual autobiography of a unique African American religious. USCC Office for Publishing and Promotion Services, Video No. 491-0, 50 minutes, $29.95. Call 1-800-235-8722 to order.

The Gift of Katharine Drexel: the life of the foundress of the Sisters of the Blessed Sacrament; highlights her ministry to African Americans and Native Americans. Bureau of Catholic Indian Missions , 2021 H Street N.W., Washington, D.C. 20006. Offering: $20.00. Also available for purchases or rent from: Franciscan Communications, 1229 S. Santee St., Los Angeles, California 90015. Call 1-800-421-8510 to order.

A Time for Miracles: The Life of Elizabeth Ann Seton, First American-born Saint. This program appeared on network television and the video is available in many video rental stores.

Kateri Tekawitha: a book on the life of the first Native-American to be beatified; by F.X. Weiser, SJ; Kateri Center, Caughnawaga, P.Q. Canada.

Mother Teresa: an account of the life and work of a remarkable woman of our time whose dedication to the poor and love of God are an inspiration to all. Videotape, Petrie Productions. Available from: Red Rose Gallery, $19.95. Call 1-800-451-5683 to order.

. . . . .

COLLEGE/YOUNG ADULT
SESSION ONE

"I Came..."

By Donald R. McCrabb
Executive Director
Catholic Campus Ministry Association

> Jesus came to provide the ultimate answer to the yearning for life and for the infinite which his heavenly Father had poured into our hearts when he created us.
>
> Pope John Paul II
> World Youth Day Address 1993

The following sessions and day of renewal on page 45 have been written with the college student and young adult in mind. These people, ranging from 18 to 30, have a wide variety of life experience. Some are full-time students pursuing a demanding career. Others are married and are trying to establish their family. Still others are single and are searching for some direction in their life.

The intent of these faith-sharing opportunities is to provide a space and time when people can come together to share their faith. The work of the pastoral leader in this situation is to create an environment which helps people open themselves to one another and to the movement of the Spirit.

This sharing of faith in Jesus Christ, his person, message, Church, and sacraments, is an act of evangelization. Jesus calls us to receive the gift of salvation from sin and to announce the good news of his kingdom of divine love, justice, and mercy. Under the power and guidance of the Holy Spirit, we strive to make God's kingdom become a reality in our families, neighborhoods, and culture.

Scriptural Focus: "I came so that they might have life and have it more abundantly" (Jn 10:10).
Catechetical Theme: Life lived in relationship with others is life worth living.
Audience: College Students and Young Adults

Objectives

1. To explore what our own experience of relationship can teach us about the ingredients of true friendship.

2. To ponder how Jesus approached his relationships.

3. To recommit ourselves to a deeper relationship with Jesus.

Preparation

Recruit a person to do a 15 minute talk on "Ingredients for Authentic Friendship" by having him/her read the following stories from Scripture:
- Luke 5: 1-11 - Jesus meets Peter.
- Luke 10: 38-42 - The Mary and Martha story.
- Mark 9: 33-37 - Jesus and the disciples.
- Matthew 18: 15-18 - When a friend wrongs you.
- Matthew 8: 5-13 - The Centurion's Servant.
- Matthew 19: 16-30 - The Rich Young Man.

Ask him or her to identify three to seven ingredients for friendship present in Jesus' relationships. Give the person enough time to write out his/her thoughts and review them with another (the pastoral leader, mentor, professor, etc.) to assure authenticity

(the ingredient emerges from Scripture) and clarity. Some points that could be covered are:

- It is hard to reach out to others; especially people we would like to know better.

- Friendship can only develop when people are willing to share what is in their heart with one another.

- It is easy to fall in love with someone. The challenge is how to stay in love.

- Jesus is the best example for us in learning how to love other people; specially when they hurt us (Mt 18:15-18).

- In the Last Supper Discourse, (Jn 13, 17) we see the depth of Jesus' intimate and loving relationship with his Father. He shows us the quality and depth of love we should have with God our Father. In the Our Father, Jesus teaches us how to pray to God our Father.

- Confrontation is never easy but it the only way we have to "clear the air" to be friends again (Mt 18: 21-35).

- In addition to forgiveness, relationships also need boundaries (Mt 8:5-13).

- One of the major themes of Vatican II is the Church as *Communio*. The original *Communio* is the relationship of the members of the Holy Trinity to one another. Through Jesus Christ, the Holy Trinity offers the world the gift of *Communio* in the Church. This is a divine reality, presented to us as gift of love. We are called to accept this *Communio* in faith and, by God's grace, realize it in our personal life and relationships. St. Paul outlines fourteen specifications of divine love which make *Communio* in this life possible. (Read I Cor 13:1-13.)

Session Outline

1. *Gathering Experience.* For groups that know each other, call the group together and introduce the topic. For groups that do not know each other, take fifteen minutes for introductions by arranging the group in a circle according to birthday. For larger groups, people can gather by their birth month. Invite people to share their name, why they came, and their hope for the time together.

2. *Reflection Experience.* Distribute the following reflection questions. Give people ten minutes to consider the questions. Encourage them to write out their responses. Be clear that no one has to share anything that is uncomfortable for them. Play instrumental music to shape this reflective time.

Recall different experiences when you felt attracted to another person. What did you do? What did you want to do?

Recall times when you felt accepted by another person. How did you feel? What did you do? What do you wish you had done?

Is a friend someone who always accepts you and always wants to be with you?

How would you describe your relationship with Jesus Christ, his Father, and the Holy Spirit?

3. *Sharing Experience.* Divide into triads; share reflections.

4. *Witness Talk.* Ingredients for Authentic Friendship. Meditate on Vatican II's teaching about divine communio as the gift of love that calls us to the deepest possible relationship with God, self, and others.

How clearly have we seen the role of the gift of divine communio received from Christ in the Church and in the sacraments and our prayer?

How have we connected this teaching of faith to our relationships to ourselves, others, and God?

5. *Friendship Ingredients.* After the talk, break into triads (different than before) and identify the ingredients for true friendship. Have the groups write out the ingredients for friendship on newsprint and post them around the room. At break time, people can get something to drink, etc. while they are reading the "the ingredients."

6. *Personal Renewal.* Invite people to center themselves, to think about their friendships with God, self, and others and decide on one or two "ingredients" that they need to work on over the next two weeks. They can write these down (only they will see them) and put them in their wallet.

7. *Closing Prayer.*
- Gathering Song: World Youth Day Song
- Gospel: John 15: 13-15
- Personal Reflection
- Prayers for Friends (petitions)
- Our Father
- Sharing of Peace
- Dismissal

Opportunities and Enhancements

1. The person giving the witness talk should be a young adult or college student. However, some groups may be better served by having a guest give this witness talk.

2. If time permits, the session could end with the celebration of the Eucharist rather than the prayer service.

3. This session was designed for an evening meeting. It should last roughly two hours. Offer it during "ordinary" young adult time; a week-day evening or late afternoon for college students.

4. This session deals with basic Christian themes; it could be an ecumenical experience.

5. Invite everyone to reflect on the "ingredients of friendship" found in the scripture passages. Publish them and invite comment.

6. View a contemporary movie (*Children of a Lesser God, Prince of Tides, Grand Canyon*) and critique it in light of the "ingredients for friendship" developed by the group.

Selected Annotated Bibliography

Marrying Well by Jim and Evelyn Whitehead (Doubleday, 1981), is an excellent overview of the many issues involved in a relationship moving toward permanent commitment within the Catholic community and tradition.

You Just Don't Understand by Deborah Tannen (William Morrow, 1990), is an analysis of the different ways men and women communicate.

Making Choices, Finding Black and White in a World of Grays by Peter Kreeft (Servant Books, Ann Arbor, Michigan, 1990) offers practical wisdom for everyday moral decisions in the light of Catholic teaching.

· · · · ·

COLLEGE/YOUNG ADULT SESSION TWO

"So That They Might Have Life. . ."

By Donald R. McCrabb
Executive Director
Catholic Campus Ministry Association

> In fact the life of each of us was thought of and willed by God before the world began, and we can rightly repeat with the Psalmist, 'O Lord, you have probed me and know me. . . truly you have formed my inmost being; you knew me in my mother's womb'" (Ps 139).
>
> Pope John Paul II
> World Youth Day Address 1993

Scriptural Focus: "I came so that they might have life and have it more abundantly" (Jn 10:10).
Catechetical Theme: Jesus offers real life.
Audience: College Students and Young Adults

Objectives

1. To explore the ways young adults and college students give life.

2. To uncover the meanings people give to the work they do or are preparing to do.

3. To learn the connection between a person's work and social responsibility.

4. To learn how to witness the moral and spiritual teachings of Jesus Christ and the Church in our personal lives and in the social, political, and economic realms.

Preparation

1. Recruit two pastoral leaders (preferably a male and female team) to facilitate the group process and offer two reflection talks.

Affirmation Talk

This talk builds on the first reflection exercise.

a. It needs to stress that young adults give life now, in their friendships, in the work they do, and even in their studies.

b. In faith we praise God for the gifts and talents we have received. Even more we thank Jesus Christ for redeeming us from the sins that both blocked our receiving divine life as well as using our talents for the service of others. Through the Church and the sacraments, we receive the divine life of saving grace which makes possible our fullest development as human beings. Through us the Holy Spirit works in the hearts of others to open them to infinite love and salvation.

c. Young adults can see the life they give as expressions of the virtues of faith, charity, and hope.

d. One way young adults demonstrate the virtue of hope is in their idealism, their desire to create a better world, their anticipation and preparation for the "generative life."

e. This talk needs to be affirming and personal. By ending with a reflection on hope as one of the virtues young adults embody, the talk will lead into the next reflection exercise.

The best way to evoke hope in others is to dwell on the mercy of God. Divine forgiveness liberates us from our past, points us toward a goal and provides the power of the Holy Spirit to get there. Nothing frees us more for a future than the assurance in faith that God has forgiven us our sins and failures. In turn, we must learn to accept God's forgiveness and extend that forgiveness to everyone in our life. We should take advantage of the sacrament of reconciliation to let Jesus Christ heal our relationships with God, self, and others. Forgiveness is the real key to hope.

Good Samaritan Reflection (Lk 10:25-37)

This talk presents the ideal life to which we are called as Christians. The following are some of the points that need to be stressed.

a. The attitude behind the Samaritan's action. He does not seek out the victim in order to do good, but he has the largeness of heart to see beyond religious and cultural differences to be moved to compassion and act.

b. The attitude toward neighbor that the community of believers has tried to cultivate over the centuries affirms the dignity of each human being before God, the possibility of justice among people, and the divine value of compassion.

c. The question before us everyday is "Who is my neighbor?"

d. There is a radical unity between the great commandments. Love of God is love of neighbor and self. Love of neighbor is love of God and self. Love of self (true love of self) is love of God and neighbor. One will always lead us to the other two. The talk needs to end by leading into the final exercise, "Who is my neighbor?"

2. Recruit a lector to proclaim the Gospel.

Session Outline

1. *Gathering Experience.* Use an experience that assures that everyone has a chance to meet each other.

2. *Brainstorming.* Using the metaphor of the life cycle of plants, have the people brainstorm ways they plant, water, fertilize, prune, and harvest "life" in their everyday lives. If the group is smaller than twenty, stay in one group. Over twenty, break into small groups of five-seven people.

Reporting: If there is one group, have someone record the responses on newsprint. If small groups are used, they will need a recorder who reports to the larger group. Ask people not to repeat items once they are mentioned.

3. *Affirmation Talk.* After the brainstorming and reporting has been done, the pastoral leader gives the affirmation talk.

4. *Personal Reflection.* After the talk, a pastoral leader notes the transition from life today to how we want to give life in the future. Invite people to image how they will give life in ten years. This is good journal material. Define this period of time (ten minutes) with instrumental music. Make sure they understand that the life they are offering to others is a personal witness based upon one's deep relation-

ship with Jesus Christ in prayer and the sacraments. Our approach to others should always have an evangelizing attitude. This means we consider ourselves the instruments of the Holy Spirit in touching the hearts and lives of others to bring them closer to God and the real goal of their lives. The life is God's life. We are the humble messengers. The result is salvation from all that diminishes others, above all from sin.

5. *Proclamation of the Gospel* (Lk 10:25-37). Once the music has ended, turn the lights down except for the place where the Gospel will be proclaimed. Bring a candle forward (if appropriate, the Easter candle) and light it in silence. The lector should come forward in silence, proclaim the Gospel, and return in silence.

6. *Gospel Reflection.* After a pause for personal reflection, the pastoral leader gives the Gospel reflection.

7. *"Who is My Neighbor?" Exercise.* Have groups of five to seven answer the following questions:

  • Whom do I "pass-by" every day that is hurting?
  • What do they need immediately?
  • What do they need over time?
  • How can we help these people?
  • How can I help these people?

The group should propose two or three ways they can help their neighbor. These could be new efforts or supportive of current efforts such as the Saint Vincent De Paul Society, Bread for the World, Habitat for Humanity or an environmental project. The pastoral leaders can help the group act on the proposals.

8. *Closing Prayer.*

  Gathering: People gather around the Christ candle.

  Gospel: Luke 10: 36-37.

  Petitions: Prayers for the Neighbors we have passed-by.

  Song of Commitment: Such as Here I Am Lord by J. Foley

  Our Father: Join hands

  Closing and Departure: Sign of Peace

Opportunities and Enhancements

1. The pastoral leader could team with a guest minister (vocation ministers, the local bishop, etc.).

2. A flutist could provide the instrumental music. Some of the Native-American flute music is conducive to reflection.

3. A larger group may allow for the acting out of the Gospel. Three people in combined roles: a narrator who becomes the priest and scribe in the parable, the scribe who becomes the victim in the parable, and Jesus who becomes the samaritan in the parable. These people would take the Scripture to write the script. They can use simple movement and lighting to change from the dialogue to the parable and back again.

4. Service groups, such as the Saint Vincent De Paul Society, and religious congregations could sponsor this session in parishes or on campuses where a formal ministry has not been developed.

Selected Annotated Bibliography

Catholic Social Teaching: Our Best Kept Secret by Peter Henriot, Edward DeBerri & Michael Schultheis (Center for Concern, 1987) situates the social teachings of the Catholic Church and summarizes the official documents.

On Human Work (Laborem Exercens) by Pope John Paul II (USCC, 1981, Pub. No. 825-8) provides an anthropology, philosophy, theology, and spirituality on work.

The Gospel on Campus edited by Michael Galligan-Stierle (USCC, 1991, Pub. No. 437-6) is a handbook of programs and resources which provides practical suggestions on the six aspects of campus ministry.

Marketplace Prophets, a highly praised videotape portrayal of 100 years of Catholic social teaching from the 1891 encyclical, *Rerum Novarum,* to the groups and individuals working for social justice today. Video No. 427-9, 60 minutes, with discussion guide. USCC, 1991.

• • • • •

RETREAT/DAYS OF REFLECTION

RETREAT/JUNIOR HIGH

The Incarnation as Invitation

By Carole M. Eipers, D. Min.
Director of Religious Education
Archdiocese of Chicago

> In fact the life of each of us was thought of and willed by God before the world began, and we can rightly repeat with the Psalmist, 'O Lord, you have probed me and know me. . . truly you have formed my inmost being; you knew me in my mother's womb' (Ps 139).

Pope John Paul II
World Youth Day Address 1993

Retreat Experience for Junior High Youth

Scriptural Focus: "I came so that they might have life and have it more abundantly" (Jn 10:10).
Catechetical Theme: In the incarnation Jesus offers real life.

Retreat Movements

1. To point out the graces received through Christ's humanity.

2. To identify and affirm the goodness of human persons and experiences, including ourselves.

3. To compare/contrast "abundant life" as lived and proclaimed by Jesus with the "good life" as proposed by contemporary society.

4. To explore and share ways in which we have and respond to Jesus' offer of abundant life.

5. To name ways in which we are and can be a source of life for others.

Preparation

Personnel: The preparation of those responsible for the direction and facilitation of the retreat is key to its effectiveness. A preparation session would include going through the process and materials, setting timeline, clarifying roles and outcomes expected in the various segments of the retreat. (e.g. "As facilitator of the small group discussion, be sure that your group outlines 3 examples to share with the large group) Assign specific roles for segment openings, prayer, etc. Participants in this session

(Paul Henderson)

would include: Catechetical leaders (DREs, Youth Ministers, Junior High Catechists, guest retreat director, etc.) and Small group facilitators (one for every 6-8 junior high people). These facilitators might be parents, parish/school staff members, parish/community leaders, college students or young adults. If the junior high people have participated in retreats previously, their own might also be facilitators. Other personnel might include adult volunteers to assist with set-up, meals, other needs.

Setting: A "place apart" from the regular classroom or religious education setting is appropriate for a retreat experience: retreat house, local campus, parish facility, etc. The environment should be conducive for private reflection, small group processes and large group sharing. The retreat experience begins with welcoming participants, making sure they feel at home with the adult participants and the facility.

Materials:
- Nametags for each participant/facilitator, etc. (color coded for small groups of 6-8).

- Tape Player - Tape of World Youth Day Song, other tapes for prayer/reflection, etc.

- Bibles - one for each participant and facilitator.

- Sets of Markers/tablets/newsprint (large) -one for each small group.

- Mural Paper - (large enough to be used by all participants during each segment of retreat.

- Magazines/newspapers for Segment D.

- Oil

- World Youth Day Pin, a poster or other symbol to be presented to each participant at Closing Ritual.

- Have participants bring their own musical instruments for prayer times, etc.

- Videos/VCR (Optional)

Retreat

Segment A.: Introduction

1. *Explain the purpose of a retreat:* a time to reflect on life, share faith, pray, decide what kind of Christians we want to be and set goals for our growth as disciples.

2. *Articulate your expectations of the group:* e.g. respectful listening to one another, participation (personal sharing should always be optional) etc. Ask participants/facilitators to share their expectations of one another.

3. *The theme of the retreat* is taken from the World Youth Day Song. Play the tape, ask participants/facilitators to listen to the words and to pick out one word or phrase which captures their hopes for this retreat. Have them write their words/phrases on the mural paper.

4. *Opening Prayer:*
- Proclaim Gospel of John 10:10-15.
- Have participants word their hopes for the retreat day in the form of a petition. (A simple form would be "God, I ask. . ." Response: "Grant our hope, Lord.") "Our God, we believe Jesus came so that we might have life. We believe you care for us and listen to our prayers and so we place our hopes for this retreat before you: (Participants voice petitions)
- We ask these things in the name of Jesus Christ, Your Son our Lord, who lives and reigns with you forever and ever. Amen."
- "Let us begin our retreat by extending a gesture of peace to one another."
- End with World Youth Day Song or other appropriate song.

Segment B: Jesus is both divine and human. Our purpose here is to get to know more about his humanity.

1. Invite participants to name the ways in which they get to know a person; e.g., what other people say; how others react; what the person herself/himself says; what the person does; and spending time and speaking with the person.

2. Small groups will engage in a Scripture search to find out all they can about Jesus. Each group will approach the search from one of the above perspectives a-d.

3. Small groups gather together to share their insights from the Scripture. Their reports may be done in poetry, drama, song, rap, drawings, or verbal reports.

4. Allow quiet time for participants to engage in the other way of getting to know Jesus, by speaking and listening in prayer.

5. Give each participant a reflection sheet with the following sections: "I know Jesus is human because" and "I know Jesus is human like me because." Allow additional time for participants to use the sheet to record their insights.

6. Gather the group. Ask participants to choose the word/phrases/quotes, etc. which captures Jesus' humanity best for them. Invite them to put their

word, phrase on the mural. Those who wish can share the reasons for their choice.

7. Present a catechesis on the teaching about the identity of Jesus. He is a divine person, the second person of the Blessed Trinity and Son of God. He has two natures, a divine and a human one. When we speak of his humanity, we mean his human nature. We affirm our faith in him as God, when we refer both to his divine nature and his divine personhood. Because of his divine nature and divine personhood, he can communicate through his humanity the abundant, divine life, which saves, renews, and energizes us. We touch and receive that divine life through our faith acceptance of and response to his gift.

Segment C: The goodness of human persons - ourselves and others.

The transition from Segment B is the Scripture, "I came so that they might have life and have it more abundantly" (Jn 10:10). Jesus came to bring us divine life. This life of grace is the source and cause of human goodness. Christ's saving work in his life, death, resurrection, and sending of the Spirit gives us the Church and the sacraments as ways to receive his abundant life. Through our acts of faith, love, and concern, the Holy Spirit brings this life to others. Examples of life-giving people help us to see how God works through us in this world.

1. Open this segment with a story of a life-giving person. It may be a personal experience, a story of a Catholic ethnic/cultural heroine/hero, a video clip, etc.

2. Give participants a time to reflect on people who have brought life to family, school/parish, community/city, nation/world. After reflection, group participants according to the arena in which their life-giver had made a contribution.

3. Small groups share the stories of the life-giving people. After they have done this, their task is to summarize the qualities, gifts, talents, characteristics of the life-givers whom they have named.

4. Gather groups together. Each group reports their summary of life-givers' qualities, etc. Add the key words/phrases from each summary to the mural.

5. As a large group, discuss how the qualities, etc. listed compare with what we know about the person Jesus.

6. Give participants time alone to consider which of the named qualities, etc. are their own strengths. If the participants know one another well enough, give them a class list on which they can write others' strengths.

7. Gather together. Title the next section of the mural "We are a gifted community." Have participants add their gifts to the mural.

8. The wrap up for this segment is to affirm the gifts and the goodness of the participants and all human persons. Above all we praise and thank God for the gifts of goodness we perceive in ourselves and others. In faith we affirm that God's grace makes possible all human goodness.

Segment D

Note to Catechetical Leader: We contrast here the "abundant life" offered by Jesus with what society calls the good life. The Son of God became human to save us from our sins which prevent us from sharing in the divine life. His redemptive action made it possible for us to have abundant life. The goodness and giftedness of human persons is a grace of God and is made visible in those people who are life-giving to others.

Our society has elements which encourage us to use our God given talents to bring "abundant life" to others. Our society also has elements which tempt us to selfishly pursue "the good life" without concern for others. Ask participants to consider:

1. From what we know about Jesus and from what we have shared about other people who are life givers, how they would define what Jesus meant by "abundant life." Title new section on mural "The Abundant Life." Allow time for reflection, re-reading of all that has been written on the mural.

2. Invite participants to add their definitions of "the abundant life" to the mural.

3. Small groups use newspapers and magazines to find examples of "the good life" which elements of society try to sell us. Each group titles a sheet of newsprint "the good life" and uses words, drawings, symbols, actual ads/stories, etc. to make their statement on what "the good life" is.

4. Groups gather together to share their descriptions of "the good life."

5. Billions of dollars are spent on selling "the good life." How can we "sell" the abundant life which Jesus offers to others? Small groups work on designing an ad, commercial, flyer, etc. that sells "abundant life" as opposed to "the good life."

6. Groups gather to share ads.

7. Quiet time for private reflection: Which appeals to you - the "abundant life" or "the good life"? Which are you spending your time and your gifts to purchase? Do you wish to make any changes? How will you begin?

8. Optional sharing at end of quiet time.

Segment E: Responding to Jesus' offer of abundant life/sharing that life with others.

1. Begin by proclaiming the Scripture passage: Lk 4:14-21. In this passage Jesus tells us something of how we can use our gifts, as he did, to bring abundant life to others. Have one sheet of newsprint for each dimension of the mission Jesus names: "glad tidings to the poor," "liberty to captives," "sight to the blind," "release to prisoners." Ask each small group to choose one of the dimensions of the mission.

2. Small groups first discuss the "audience" section of their mission, e.g. who are the "poor" in our school? Who are the "captives" in our community? Who are the "blind" in our parish?

3. After their "audience" has been named, they consider their mission. For example, the poor in our school are those without friends; we can be "glad tidings" to them by_____.

4. Small groups bring their reports back to the large group. Their presentation can be in any form, but should include a summary of the individuals/ groups whom they have identified and the ways in which a junior high person can carry on the mission of Jesus to these people.

5. Quiet time for personal reflection on these questions: How do my gifts fit the mission of Jesus? To whom can I best bring life? How will I do it?

6. Extend the reflection time to allow optional sharing with a friend.

7. Optional sharing with large groups and/or wrap up.

Segment F: Closing Ritual

1. List on newsprint the parts of the closing ritual: environment, opening music (song), opening prayer, scripture reading, response and/or reflection, ritual (and presentation of symbol), gesture of peace, final prayer or blessing, and song.

2. Have individuals choose which part of the prayer they would like to prepare. A facilitator should assist each group.

3. Celebrate closing prayer.

Suggestions for Using This Retreat Model

Schedule Adaptations

1. Partial or half day retreats - Segments can be used separately for a series of shorter retreat

experiences. Small group activities can take place in the large group and/or some of the activities can be done prior to the retreat in order to conserve time.

2. Extended Retreat (two days and/or one night)
   a. Procession to retreat location as a sign of our unity with all youth who will be participating in World Youth Day events this year.
   b. In Segment B, use a video on Jesus' life prior to the scripture search.
   c. For Segment C, groups might prepare a video/ slide show/photo display highlighting people who "came so that others might have life." Another option is to have participants name life-giving people in their families, parish, school, or community and invite them to share their stories at the retreat.
   d. In segment D, instead of using magazines and newspapers, small groups could go into the neighborhood on a "scavenger hunt" to find signs of "the abundant life" and the contrasting "the good life."

Resources

Videos: *Awakenings* (life, quality of life) or *The Chosen* (relationships). Both can be rented fron video rental stores.

Catholic ethnic leaders who can witness to the ways in which their culture lives, fosters, and celebrates Christian values which bring "abundant life."

Mother Teresa, Love, A Fruit Always in Season; Dorothy Hunt, ed,. (San Francisco: Ignatius Press, 1987).

Mother Teresa: an account of the life and work of a remarkable woman of our time whose dedication to the poor and love of God are an inspiration to all. Videotape, Petrie Productions. Available from: Red Rose Gallery, $19.95. Call 1-800-451-5683 to order.

. . . . .

RETREAT/SENIOR HIGH

You Cannot Serve Both God and Consumerism

By Rev. James DiGiacomo, SJ
High School Religion Teacher
Regis High School, New York, New York

In fact the life of each of us was thought of and willed by God before the world began, and we can rightly repeat with the Psalmist, 'O Lord, you have probed me and know me. . . truly you have formed my inmost being; you knew me in my mother's womb' (Ps 139).

Pope John Paul II
World Youth Day Address 1993

Scriptural Focus: "I came so that they might have life and have it more abundantly" (Jn 10:10).
Catechetical Theme: Jesus offers real life.
Catechetical Plan: A Day of Recollection for Senior High Age Group

Preparation

These materials assume that those in charge of this Day of Reflection have prepared the materials, times, suitable setting, and have thought through the schedule, expectations, and prayerful outcome.

The three reflections in this material provide you with a progressive lead into the teaching of Jesus about real life and the challenge that comes from consumerism in our culture.

Introduction

This is a different kind of day of recollection. It asks the participants not to step aside from everyday life, but to look at it more closely and see it the way they never did before. If they do, they can come away with a new awareness of themselves and of their world, and maybe even come away with a desire for a fuller life.

Just as catechumens in the Roman empire had to choose between Christianity and the Roman way of life, young Americans today must confront many points of tension between America's dominant culture and the following of Jesus Christ. This program analyzes the consumerism and materialism which spawn excessive competition, promiscuity, and lack of compassion, and presents Christianity as an alternative vision of life — one that is more genuine and honest and ultimately more fulfilling.

A Major Challenge From Our Culture (Retreat Leader Input)

Consumer Culture

Consumerism is so pervasive and so close to us that we have to step back and examine it from several perspectives to grasp its impact on us, our hopes and dreams and fears.

Consumerism is not only a preoccupation with buying consumer goods, but it is also a whole way of life that defines us in terms of what we possess and consume. In this worldview, possessions, pleasure, power, and prestige are not mere adornments of the self but constitute the very self. An ad for Cadillac said, "You are what you drive." Bumper stickers proclaim "Born to shop" and "A woman's place is in the mall." At the dedication of a new mall, a congressman said, in all seriousness:

> We are gathered here today not merely to dedicate a shopping mall, but to rededicate ourselves, mind and body, to the spirit of consumerism and to seek an ever more deeply indebted relationship to the process of purchasing merchandise.[1]

A nationwide survey of incoming college freshmen in 1988 [2] revealed that 76 percent considered "being very well off financially" a very important goal of education, up from 39 percent in 1970. At the same time, only 39 per cent thought that developing a meaningful philosophy of life was important, down from 83 percent in 1966. A high school junior, commenting on this survey, wrote: "The way the world is now, being well off should be an important thing. A meaningful philosophy of life cannot help you in the real world." A classmate observed: "Isn't this true of most of society? Everyone is concerned with monetary gains, their main motivation throughout life. We all (that is, most of us) have one basic goal in life: to look good, eat good, and smell good."

Does television inculcate these values? A high school freshman girl told an interviewer, "Alexis (of *Dynasty*) is bad. Like she's evil. She's vicious and bold and glamorous. And she's everything that any woman could want to be. . . .. She gets whatever she wants." A boy in her class observed: "I sort of admire J.R. Ewing (of *Dallas*), the way he can just corrupt everybody and not even let it affect him."[3]

Summing Up

Consumer Values	Christian Values
Getting	The worth of a person cannot
Owning	be measured by the money or
Enjoying	the things he/she own.
Producing	
Competing	Frugality is to be preferred
Winning	to conspicuous consumption.
.... which put	
stress on	We are responsible for one another.
Aggressiveness	
Self-satisfaction	Justice and honesty are not to
Status	be compromised in the struggle
Security	for status and security.

(Paul Henderson)

The Role Of Advertising

The following two videos show how advertising makes consumerism such a force in our lives. These videos are well worth seeing. They can be purchased or rented.

Still Killing Us Softly; Starring Jean Kilbourne; Cambridge Documentary Films; P.O. Box 385; Cambridge, Mass. 02139. Call 1-617-354-3677 to order.

Advertising is one of the most powerful educational tools in our society. It is the propaganda of consumer culture. It tells us: Be consumers. Happiness can be bought. Products can fulfill us and satisfy our deepest human needs.

Advertisements influence our attitudes; our attitudes shape and determine our behavior. Ads sell not only products but also values; images; and concepts of love, sex, romance, success, popularity, and normalcy. They tell us who we are and what we should be.

The 30-Second Dream, a montage of visual and sound images from television commercials, shows how advertisers skillfully play on fears of inadequacy and fantasies of wish-fulfillment in four essential areas: Family, Intimacy, Vitality, and Success.

Commenting on these ads' underlying theme, Erich Fromm said "It is the general fear of not being loved, and then to be able, by some product, to be loved."

The 30-Second Dream; Mass Media Ministries; 2116 North Charles St.; Baltimore, Md. 21218. Call 1-301-727-3677 to order.

Some Consequences Of Consumerism

Consumer culture's dominant myth is: You should experience whatever you desire, own whatever you want, and relate intimately with whomever you wish.[4]

This implicit, taken-for-granted, uncritically accepted viewpoint underlines much of the hedonism, the greed, and the sexual irresponsibility that plague our society. As one high school student wrote. "The society in which we live is centered around two ideals: sex and money. The two work hand in hand. Sex is used to make money, and money is used to get sex. These values are so instilled in our mind today that it's impossible to deter teenagers from having sex."

Relating Scripture to This Challenge (Retreat Leader Input)

Jesus on Consumerism

No one can serve two masters. He will either hate one and love the other, or be devoted to one and despise the other. You cannot serve God and mammon" (Mt 6:24).

So do not worry and say: "What are we to eat?" or "What are we to drink?" or "What are we to wear? All these thing the pagans seek. Your heavenly Father knows that you need them all. Seek first the kingdom (of God) and his righteousness, and all these things will be given you besides." (Mt 6:31-33).

. . . Take care to guard against all greed, for though one may be rich, one's life does not consist of possessions. (Lk 12:15).

The Pedagogy of Jesus. Jesus never denies or ignores our basic human needs for security, affection, acceptance, growth. But he shows, by word and sign, how these include a need for something greater. Thus, in the sixth chapter of John's Gospel, after feeding the crowd with the loaves and fish, he points out that mere bread can never satisfy their deeper hunger. Only the Eucharist, the Bread of Life, can do that, ". . . You were looking for me. . . because you ate the loaves and were filled. Do not work for food that perished but for the food that endures for eternal life" (Jn 6:26-27).

The mass media describe a world in which self-indulgence is the ideal and in which conspicuous consumption guarantees fulfillment. They teach us to love things and use people. Jesus, on the other hand, tells us we are created to love people and use things.

He is not against our having things and enjoying them. But he reminds us that they can never satisfy our deepest cravings for the fullness of life which is nothing less than God.

Role-Play Exercise

Read the story of Zaccheus, Lk 19:1-10. Zaccheus has given away half of his possessions to the poor and repaid four times anyone he has cheated. Jesus has converted him to a simpler lifestyle. Image that his wife's name is "Zelda" and his son is "Irving." Act out their response to his conversion and the impact on their lives. For example, Irving is in his third year at "Jericho Prep" at 200 drachmas a year. Now he will have to transfer to Jericho Public High School, where they are busing in Samaritan students. Will Zaccheus stick to his resolution? Should he?

For Discussion

What do you want out of life besides "to look good, eat good, and smell good"? How do you plan to get it?

Is Jesus' attitude toward money and possessions realistic? How can he expect us not to worry?

Jesus says our life does not depend on possessions. Well, then, what does it depend on?

Prayer Service

Group:

Do not store up treasures for yourself here on earth, where moth and decay destroy, and thieves break in and steal.But store up treasures in heaven, where neither moth or decay destroys, nor thieves break in and steal. For where your treasure is, there also will your heart be (Mt. 6:19-21).

Leader:

Heavenly Father, help us to see the world with the eyes of faith, so that we may set our hearts on what truly matters in your sight. We ask this Jesus Christ, your Son and our Brother.
R. Amen.

Reader:

A reading from the holy Gospel according to Luke:(Lk 12:16-21).

Psalm 121 (Group recites alternate verses)
I lift up my eyes toward the mountains;
    whence shall help come to me?
My help is from the Lord,
    who made heaven and earth.

May he not suffer your foot to slip;
    may he slumber not who guards you:
Indeed he neither slumber nor sleeps,
    the guardian of Israel.

The Lord is your guardian; the Lord is your shade;
    he is beside you at your right hand.
The sun shall not harm you by day,
    nor the moon by night.

The Lord will guard you from all evil;
    he will guard your life.
The Lord will guard your coming and your going,
    both now and forever.

Leader:

Let us pray. Lord, give us the wisdom to be rich in your sight. May we always trust in your protection, and thus come into the kingdom you have prepared for those who love you. We ask this through Christ our Lord.
R. Amen.

Notes

1. Betz, M., *Making Life Choices,* Paulist Press, 1992, pp. 58-59.

2. Carmody, D., "To Freshmen, A Big Goal Is Wealth," *N.Y. Times,* Jan. 14, 1988.

3. London, H., "What TV Drama is Teaching Our Children," *N.Y. Times,* Aug. 23, 1987.

4. Fowler, J., *Stages of Faith,* Harper & Row, 1981, pp. 20.

. . . . .

COLLEGE/YOUNG ADULT RETREAT

"Life Abundant..."

By Donald R. McCrabb
Executive Director
Catholic Campus Ministry Association

> Jesus came to meet men and women, to heal the sick and the suffering, to free those possessed by devils and to raise the dead: he gave himself on the Cross and rose again from the dead, revealing that his is the Lord of life: the author and source of Life without end.
>
> Pope John Paul II
> World Youth Day Address 1993

Day of Renewal

Scriptural Focus: "I came that they might have life and have it more abundantly" (Jn 10:10).
Catechetical Theme: To live fully is to pour out one's life for others.
Audience: College Students and Young Adults

Objectives

1. To identify and reflect on the experience of being pulled in many different directions.

2. To explore how sacrifice and selflessness are part of being centered.

3. To reflect on the direction Jesus took in his life.

4. To consider if the direction of my life is a promise "of life, life abundant," the life of grace, the life in the Holy Spirit.

Preparation

1. Limit the group to thirty people. Multiple days could be scheduled to accommodate larger groups and diverse schedules. This experience needs at least twelve participants. They should bring their Bible and something in which to journal.

2. One of the pastoral leaders or young adult leaders need to be recruited to do a suffering talk which needs to include the following:

- Sharing their centering experience (See Centering Exercise below.).

- Identifying in that experience any suffering (discipline, endurance, pain, etc.) connected with it and any selflessness (self-gratification was not the sole and exclusive motivation).

- Reflection on suffering: that there are a lot of different types of suffering and that we tend to image suffering in very dramatic ways. Often, we will gladly suffer to achieve a greater good.

- Review the central role of the passion and death of Jesus in his work of salvation which brings us divine and eternal life. The major portions of all four gospels contain the passion narratives. Jesus is indeed the "Suffering Servant" who offers himself for the salvation of the world. Refer to Phil 2:2-11, a hymn that outlines the intention of the Son of God to become human, suffer, die and rise for our redemption. Note the words of Jesus about the necessity of his suffering in the divine plan, "Was it not necessary that the Messiah should suffer these things and enter into his glory?" (Lk 24:26). As disciples of Jesus, we must also face the reality of suffering as part of our Christian calling. "Whoever wishes to come after me must deny himself, take up his cross, and follow me" (Mt 16:24).

- That selflessness is best seen on a scale; rarely are we purely selfless or totally self absorbed.

- What we are willing to suffer for tells us a lot about who we are and where we really want to go.

- Avoiding pain or the threat of pain often limits our freedom. Suffering is part of life; it can either lead to more abundant life and freedom or to fear and passivity.

- The great seduction of our day is that we "should be. . . ." someone we are not (the different directions) and that any suffering, no matter the purpose, must be avoided.

Outline of Day

(Based on beginning at 10:00 am and continuing until 8:00 pm)

1. *Gathering Experience.* Invite people to gather in a circle, say their name, where they have come from (direction, place, and home town) and what burden (anxiety, overwork, or an upcoming exam), if any, they have brought with them. Welcome people in the name of the Lord and the sponsoring group (parish, campus ministry, etc) and invite the people to welcome one another.

2. *Directions for Exercise.*

   A. The pastoral leader invites the group to brainstorm in the large group all the different directions they feel "pulled." Ask people to complete the sentence: "I should really be."

   B. The pastoral leader helps the group cluster the "I should" statements. Label the statements an ism. Invite the group to come up with their own isms; conventional (consumerism, sexism, etc.) or unconventional (political correctness, perfect body-ism, etc.).

3. *Centering Exercise.* Through the use of a guided meditation, invite people to quiet themselves, relax, and to gently go back to a time in their life (either recent or long ago), when they felt centered; when they were living out of their truest self.

4. *Suffering Talk.* Have someone read Rom 8:31-39 after which the suffering talk is given. The group is broken up into small groups of three or four and invited to share with one another what in the talk rang true and what they resisted.

5. *Lunch Break.* Provide a simple lunch of soup, sandwiches, etc. Give people time to eat and go for a walk or play some group games (basketball, volley-ball, etc.).

6. *Jesus' Direction.*

  A. The pastoral leader divides the group into four. Each group takes one of the Gospels.

  B. All of the Gospels agree that the direction of Jesus' life took him to Jerusalem where he would accomplish his life's ultimate saving work through his passion, death, and resurrection. Each group is to identify all the ways in which Jesus gave love and divine life to people on the eve of his passion and during it. For example: The Last Supper; The Healing of Malchus; Paradise for the Good Thief; etc. Use only the Jerusalem-Passion narratives from the four Gospels.

  C. Each group will need a recorder who will report to the large group their findings.

  D. The pastoral leader will point out, after all groups have reported, that Jesus endured rejection, betrayal, hostility, injustice, a scourging at the pillar, a crowning with thorns, a nailing to the Cross, thirst, agony - in other words, profound suffering and death so that we might have abundant divine life, salvation, the grace of the Holy Spirit's indwelling to make us whole and holy. Our own identification with Christ means: lose the self; take the cross; follow Jesus. Then the Spirit will make us instruments of bringing divine life to others.

7. *Prayer for Direction.* People are invited to reflect quietly on the type of help they need to follow the direction of their truest self in the spirit of Jesus. These thoughts can be written in their journal and summarized in a prayer of petition that they print out on a 3 x 5 card. These are collected, shuffled, and redistributed to the group.

8. *Closing Eucharist.* Celebrate the Mass of the Day. The homily should be very brief; give plenty of time for the prayers of petition to speak. (Each person will read one.)

Selected Annotated Bibliography

The People: Reflections of Native Peoples on the Catholic Experience in North America; National Catholic Educational Association; see especially chapter VII," Practical Helps for Teachers, and Prayer Services," p. 82. (Washington, D.C.: NCEA, 1992).

Renewing the Earth: An Invitation to Reflection and Action on the Environment in the Light of Catholic Social Teaching. This 20-page pamphlet addresses global warming, depletion of the ozone layer, deforestation, and toxic and nuclear waste. (Washington, D.C.: United States Catholic Conference, 1992). Pub. No. 468-6.

· · · · ·

© 1992 WORLD YOUTH DAY, INC

PRAYER AND WORSHIP

SUGGESTIONS FOR LITURGICAL PLANNING

1. Work with your parish liturgy committee to develop a plan to help liturgies reflect the Year of Preparation throughout 1993. Some ideas might include:

While the theme of every Mass is the Paschal Mystery, the liturgy committee might plan to focus on the abundant life that is open to us through the death and resurrection of Jesus.

Regular mention of World Youth Day in the prayer of the faithful.

The assembly might be asked to contribute to a collection of items that the community might give to an organization whose work is an extension of Christ's abundant life. For example: food, clothing, items for personal hygiene, medicine, children's toys, books, crafts, letters of support, etc.

The liturgy committee might extend a special invitation to youth and young adults to become liturgical ministers in this year of preparation.

A special banner could be placed in the church reflecting the theme of the WYD, "I came so that they might have life and have it more abundantly" Jn 10:10.

Note that the gospel for the Fourth Sunday of Easter is John 10:1-10. The parish might be able to use that Sunday to focus on the WYD theme and to pray for the success of that gathering. A special blessing for those going to Denver could be given as they continue their spiritual preparation.

2. The parish might designate a specific weekend as Homecoming Sunday. A special effort could be made to invite youth and young adults back to church. This could take place prior to the Denver gathering or in the fall of 1993.

3. Consider a display in the vestibule of the church highlighting youth and young adults in the parish. The display could show ways that youth and young adults reflect the abundant life that Jesus has opened to us.

4. A series of brief reflections written by young adults or youth could be published in the parish bulletin.

5. A series of personal meditations could be published in the bulletin during the Sundays in May when the gospel readings speak of the new life that Jesus is.

6. A special prayer could be said on the first Sunday of the year to commemorate the beginning of the year of preparation.

7. Youth might distribute the WYD prayer at the entrance of the church.

· · · · ·

SUGGESTIONS FOR MUSIC

There will be a great many opportunities to use liturgical music in prayer and worship throughout the year. Of course the World Youth Day Theme song is very appropriate. Some of the songs suggested here are compatible with the WYD theme, while others are suggested because of their usefulness during pilgrimage. These songs are only suggestions. Others that are more suitable to the specific needs of a community may also be used. The songs are listed by the book in which they can be found.

Lead Me Guide Me, GIA Publications, Chicago 1987
  "Soon and Very Soon" no. 4
  "Keep Me Near the Cross" no. 45
  "Wherever He Leads, I'll Go" no. 50
  "I Know That My Redeemer Lives" no. 63*
  "Lord When You Came/Pescador de Hombres" no. 116
  "I Have Decided to Follow Jesus" no. 118
  "Spirit of the Living God" no. 126
  "I Received the Living God" no. 137
  "We've Come This Far By Faith" no. 225
  "Leaning on the Everlasting Arms" no. 257
  "Hush, Hush, Somebody's Callin' Mah Name" no. 262
  "I Want Jesus to Walk with Me" no. 263

Peoples Mass Book, World Library Publications 1984
  "Lord, Let Me Walk" no. 57
  "All You On Earth" no. 70
  "In Christ There Is No East Or West" no. 103

"The Living God" no. 113
"Christ Be Beside Me" no. 231

Gather, GIA Publications, Chicago 1988
 "Song of the Risen One" no. 181
 "Canticle of the Sun" no. 197
 "The Lord is My Life" no. 209
 "Sow the Word" no. 211
 "Alleluia Sing" no. 215
 "You Are the Voice" no. 222
 "Eye Has Not Seen" no. 275
 "You Will Show Me the Path of Life" no. 277
 "The Song of All Seed" no. 289
 "We Have Been Told" no. 296
 "We Are Called" no. 301
 "Gather Us In" no. 311
 "I Am the Bread of Life" no. 337

Glory and Praise, Comprehensive Edition, NALR, Phoenix, Arizona 1991
 "Anthem" no. 19
 "Choose Life" no. 41
 "Come To the Water" no. 56
 "Jesus is the Bread of Life" no. 123
 "City of God" no. 47
 "On Eagles Wings" no. 178
 "You Are Near" no. 272

Today's Missal, Music Issue for 1993, OCP, Portland, Oregon
 "Bread for the World Broken" no. 425
 "Center of My Life" no. 472
 "God Has Chosen Me" no. 619
 "God of Abraham" no. 478
 "Lead Me Lord" no. 600
 "Pan De Vida no. 462
 "Servant Song" no. 520
 "Song of the Body of Christ" no. 449
 "I Am the Resurrection" no. 491
 "Sing of the Lord's Goodness" no. 447
 "I am the Light of the World" no. 531
 "This Alone" no. 583

. . . . .

Homily Suggestions

Because the preparations for World Youth Day '93 will continue throughout the year, brief homily suggestions are given, in abbreviated form, for several key weekends.

Solemnity of the Epiphany of the Lord
Beginning of Year of Preparation and Outreach
January 3, 1993

RDGS 20 Isaiah 60:1-6, Ephesians 3:2-3, 5-6, Matthew 2:1-12

As this special year of preparation and pilgrimage begins, let us look to the astrologers whose own pilgrimage led them to the Christ. Their persistence, their journey, their encounter with Herod, their prayers and dreams were all part of a life-transforming experience that culminates in an encounter with God incarnate. In our own journey throughout this year of preparation, may we too be watching for encounters with the presence of God and the abundant life of Jesus.

Nineteenth Sunday in Ordinary Time
August 8, 1993
RDGS 116 1 Kings 19:9, 11-13, Romans 9:1-5, Matthew 14:22-33

Just as Elijah was told, we say to those traveling to Denver, "Go outside and stand on the mountain before the Lord; the Lord will be passing by." Pilgrims need to be watchful, for God will come to us in some unexpected ways. In the gospel we find two other directions for us as pilgrims to follow during this journey. Like Peter, our walk should be with Jesus; and like Peter, when we walk with Jesus, we can depend on him to catch us when we fall. As pilgrims, whether we are journeying to Denver or not, we all must make the time to go to the "mountain" or a holy place to be alone with God and to pray.

Assumption of the Blessed Virgin Mary
August 15, 1993
VIGIL RDGS 621 1 Chronicles 15:3-4, 15-16. 16:1-2, 1 Corinthians 15:54-57, Luke 11:27-28

Just as David and the Israelites assembled in Jerusalem, so too, young people are assembled in Denver to make a loud rejoicing for the Lord. We and all the church gather, united with them in the same Paschal meal. In the gospel, Jesus also speaks words of rejoicing. But rather than rejoice at the goodness of his mother, Jesus recalls to us our task as pilgrims, "Blest are they who hear the word of God and keep it." As pilgrims on a journey through a world of confusion and temptation, we take hope in the fact that "God has given us the victory through our Lord Jesus Christ."

DAY RDGS 622 Revelations 11:19, 12:1-6, 10 1 Corinthians 15:20-26, Luke 1:39-56

In a culture were the title "mother earth" has been given more and more reverence and respect, how fitting it is that we celebrate the Assumption of

Mary, the Mother of Abundant Life. The Assumption of Mary reminds us that all the life we see before us is but a reflection of the abundant life that Jesus, her son, has made possible for us. Listen to the charisms that are spoken of in the Canticle of Mary. The abundant life of God is both powerful and gentle. St. Paul in his letter states it so simply, "In Christ, all will come to life."

It might be appropriate to pray for all pilgrims gathered in Denver. The prayer for families and parents on page 51 can be adapted for this purpose.

25th Sunday in Ordinary Time
September 19, 1993
Catechetical Sunday
RDGS 134 Isaiah 55:6-9, Philippians 1:20-24, 27, Matthew 20:1-16

The mercy of God is beyond our understanding. It is beyond measure. Yet God's mercy offers to us great comfort and consolation. God not only calls us in mercy but calls us to be merciful. The abundant everlasting life of Christ has been opened to us and we must not withhold it from anyone. As a community we must be ever constant in our welcoming, sincere in our mercy, and vigilant against those things that separate us. As catechists we must remember that it is never too late in the day to be welcomed into God's vineyard. Let us be attentive to those things that keep our sisters and brothers from pursuing their urge to seek the Lord. For St. Paul, "life means Christ" and so as catechists we are called to make open the path to Christ's life.

30th Sunday in Ordinary Time
October 24, 1993
World Youth Day Sunday
RDGS 149 Exodus 22:20-26, 1 Thessalonians 1:5-10, Matthew 22:34-40

The justice of God shall be observed! Our God is compassionate and expects us to be the same. Throughout this special year of preparation, we have been servants to the orphans, to the poor, to the oppressed, to children, to the elderly, and to others. (Recount some of the service that youth and young adults have done in this special year of preparation.) Our call for the year has been to live life abundantly and hopefully. In spirit and action we have done that. Perhaps St. Paul's praise of the Thessalonians applies to us too, since we have turned away from the idols and allure of a material world to serve God.

· · · · ·

WORLD YOUTH DAY PRAYERS

The following prayers may be helpful to your community as you prepare for World Youth Day.

Prayer for Young People
(as they prepare for and travel to the World Youth Day)

Lord, lead me along the path of your love and keep me faithful to the journey I make.

With the fire of your Spirit illumine the road I travel and help me up when I stumble and fall.

With your Word of truth make me a faithful pilgrim and help me to choose what is right and just and true.

From your heart of love give me the grace I need to love my fellow pilgrims and to share with them your peace.

With the power of your cross teach me to pour out myself in service of the poor, that my life might be filled with your love.

From the table of your Word and your Body and Blood, nourish me with food that gives life.

Lead my steps safely along your path and gather me in with all your sons and daughters, together with our Holy Father, and all who make their way to you and the life you promise.

Grant this and all good things through Christ our Lord.

Amen.

Rev. Austin H. Fleming

Prayer for Youth
(as they prepare for and travel to the World Youth Day)

Where can I go when the night is dark and I stumble along the way?

I will go up to the house of the Lord, my God, whose light turns the night into day.

Where can I go when my heart is low and my spirit wounded with pain?

I will go up to the house of the Lord, my God, to the God who gives joy to my youth!

Where can I go when my heart is full, overflowing with thanks and praise?

I will go up to the house of the Lord, my God, whose peace is the joy of my days.

Where can I go when my heart is healed and mended with comfort and love?

I will go up to the house of the Lord, my God,
   whose grace gives me strength from above.
Where can I go when my heart is at peace and
   filled with the spirit of truth?
I will go up to the house of the Lord, my God, to the
   God who gives joy to my youth!

Where can I go to give of myself in return for all
   I've received?
I will go up to the house of the Lord, my God, who
   calls me to serve those in need.
Where can I go to pour out myself as God's love is
   poured out for all?
I will go up to the house of the Lord, my God,
   whose love bids me answer the call.
Where can I go for life worth the living, for love
   strong in word, deed, and truth?
I will go up to the house of the Lord, my God, to the
   God who gives joy to my youth!

Rev. Austin H. Fleming

Prayer of the Pilgrims' Parents
Lord, you have called our children to make a
   journey of faith,
and with the help of your Spirit they have heard and
   answered the word you have spoken in their
   hearts.
Keep them faithful to your word and hold them
   safely in the palm of your hand as they make
   their way to Denver.
Teach them to choose life and to choose what is
   right and just and true.
Help them to share with others the life you promise,
   especially in service of the poor.
Open their minds and their hearts to the truth of the
   scriptures.
Nourish them with the bread and cup of the Eucharist;
and fill them with love for our Holy Father, Pope
   John Paul II.
Lead our young pilgrims along the way, Lord, and
   make safe their journey to you and the life you
   promise us.
We ask this through Christ our Lord. Amen.

Rev. Austin H. Fleming

· · · · ·

Prayer Service

Gathering in Preparation for International World Youth Day in Denver

By Ms. Leota Roesch
Archdiocese of San Antonio
Director of Training and Formation

Theme: Jesus offers real life.
   Environment: Room is darkened or lighting is
dimmed. A large candle and the Scriptures are
placed in the center of the group who are in a single
circle in chairs or on the floor around the room.
Before you darken the room, set the environment:

1. Young people are invited to empty their hands of
   materials and to focus on the God present within
   and among them.

2. Explain the symbolism of the Candle: Christ is
   the Light of the world (from Scripture and
   strongly symbolized for us in the Easter Vigil
   liturgy). As the candle consumes itself in order
   to give us light; so did Christ use himself up
   completely for us in his passage from death to
   life in the Paschal Mystery. Have a young adult
   or youth light the candle after you've set the
   mood.

3. Help them calm themselves through breathing
   exercises, etc. Rather than just asking them to
   concentrate on their breathing, consider doing it
   in the context of prayer, mantra-wise: "I
   breathe in the Spirit of God. I breathe out the
   cares and concerns of the moment." Repeat
   several times.

Call to Prayer: Sacred Gesture

Reflective Listening: Suggested Music:
Instrumental music;

David Haas, "Song of the Body of Christ," from
   the album, *Creating God,* Copyright ©1989,
   GIA Publications, Inc., 7404 S Mason Ave.
   Chicago, IL, 60638;

Donna Peña, "Against the Grain or Contra La
   Corriente" from the album of the same name,
   Copyright ©1983, Word Inc.

Leader:
   In the Gospel according to John, Jesus proclaims:
"I came so that they may have life and have it more
abundantly." Life, for Jesus and for us, his followers, has to mean more than just the ability to breathe,
eat, walk, show our emotions, do a job, and so forth.

What is the life that Jesus offers us? First, let us listen to the "life" that some others offer us.

Person 1:

(It might be helpful to have a group of young people prepare a poster-size collage or slide show that can be on display while the following is being read. The poster could be made of advertisements from magazines aimed at young adults or teens — *Seventeen, YM, Rolling Stone,* etc.) We are "really living" if we wear the right clothes, listen to the right music, wear our hair a special way, and wash it with special products; if we are seen only with the "in crowd," if we have all the right things - money, VCR's, T.V.'s, stereos, CD players, a car, a girlfriend or boyfriend, the best condo, the right job; if we spend our time getting things, going places, and using people; if our friends are just like we are, instead of being different.

En el mundo materialista, "vivimos de verdad" si somos populares, si llevamos la ropa de última moda, escuchamos la música de MTV, nos parecemos exactamente a los modelos en los anuncios comerciales, si nuestros amigos o nuestras amigas son populares; si tenemos un buen trabajo o un apartamento; si vamos de compras, paseamos mucho y usamos a la gente para nuestro provecho; si nuestras amistades son exactamente igual que nosotros, en vez de ser "diferentes."

Person 2:

Jesus offers us life of a different sort. Listen to what the Scripture describes as true life.

Person/Persona 3:

(Several people read a Scripture passage as noted here. Please pause significantly after each reading. These are some passages that describe "life to the fullest." You may wish to choose other passages.) Mi 6:8., Mt 11:5

Person/Persona 4:

Mt 25:34-40

Person/Persona 5:

Jn 5:24; Jn 6:51

Person 2:

The life that Jesus promises us is no easy life; there are no "quick fixes." We must serve others first and with joy, be in relationship to Jesus, to his Father, and to their Holy Spirit, and we must be ready to suffer the consequences of our relationship to Jesus. The struggle to be holy is life-giving, and the life that we experience in Jesus brings peace, joy, and strength.

Leader:

Please turn to a neighbor and share with him/her (10-15 seconds with each one) what is the most difficult thing for you in living the life that Christ offers you and how you feel when you know and believe that you are living as Christ wants you to.

Intercessions:

(Invite the participants to offer prayers aloud using the following formula or one of your own choosing.)

Jesus, I wish to lead a life that is full by_____ (e.g., volunteering some of my time to help at the parish food bank; giving money that I would have spent on designer clothes to a shelter for the homeless; offering to take care of my brothers and sisters for free so that my parents can have some time for themselves, etc.).

Closing:

Close with the Our Father and the Sign of Peace.

• • • • •

Send Off/Despedida

By Ms. Leota Roesch
Archdiocese of San Antoino
Director of Training and Formation

Entrance:

Appropriate music. Those who will be making the pilgrimage to Denver enter in procession along with the pastor/bishop and adult leaders.

Opening prayer:

Let us begin in the name of the Father, and of the Son, and of the Holy Spirit. Or let us begin this celebration by signing the person on either side of us with the sign of our redemption and fullness of life. "In the name ..."

Today culminates a special year of preparation for these young people of our parish/diocese, a year of pilgrimage, a year in which they made a journey inward, first of all, to prepare their minds and hearts to be "traveling messengers of Christ" (Decree on the Laity, 14), and a year in which they have journeyed together to prepare their minds and hearts to join on a great outward pilgrimage with thousands of other young people from around the globe which will culminate in Denver and which will visibly unite them with Pope John Paul II. For several days they will celebrate their unity as a young church by participating in prayer and discussion groups, by celebrating in song, and by interacting in fellowship. As the Holy Father said in announcing the theme of the World Youth Day meeting ("I came so that they may have life and have it more abundantly" Jn 10:10.), "What better hope and task is there than to start off on a journey of discovering and encountering the presence of Jesus Christ, the source of life, of full life?"

Proclamation of the Word:

One or more young persons proclaim the Word. Suggested readings are taken from the "Order for the Blessing of Pilgrims on Their Departure," *Book of Blessings* (Collegeville: The Liturgical Press, 1989). 2 Cor 5:6-10, We are away from the Lord; Is 2:2-5, Let us walk in the light of the Lord; Lk 2:41-51, Jesus and the disciples make a pilgrimage to Jerusalem for Passover; Lk 24:13:35, The Emmaus Story; Heb. 10:19-25, the attitudes needed for this earthly pilgrimage; 1 Pt 2:4-12, We live as strangers on exile. (You may wish to choose other readings, such as Tb 5:17b-18a, 21-22, Tobit's blessing of his son and his consolation of his wife.)

Response:

Sung or recited (cf Ps. 24, 27, or the Pilgrimage Psalms 120-134.) Sung response (Donna Peña, "On Holy Ground," Copyright ©1992, 7404 S. Mason Ave. Chicago, Ill., 60638; John Michael Talbot, "On Holy Ground" from the *Be Exalted* album; Donna Peña," Digo Si," "Señor or Vengamos Cantando" from the *Contra La Corriente/Against the Grain* album, Copyright ©1989, 7404 S. Mason Ave. Chicago, Ill. 60638; Rory Cooney, "Come to Us" from the *Do Not Fear to Hope* album, Copyright © by NALR, etc.)

Homily:

Presider, using the scripture readings, stresses the tradition and purpose of pilgrimage and this unique opportunity for pilgrimage for the young church assembled.

General Intercessions:
Presider:

We are a pilgrim people and we confidently call on God from whom we come and to whom we go.

Lector/s:

Throughout salvation history, good and gracious God, you have been our guide and you are the way we follow. Protect us as we begin this pilgrimage, so that we may return home safely, let us pray. . . .

Jesus, your son promised us fullness of life. May our life's journey be marked by following him unconditionally, let us pray. . . .

As we encounter others throughout this pilgrimage, may we welcome them with hospitality and walk with them in faith, let us pray. . . .

(Other intentions as are appropriate for the gathered assembly.)

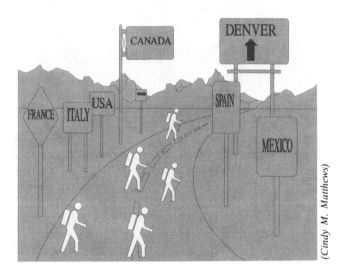

WORLD YOUTH DAY 1993

(Cindy M. Matthews)

The **Presider** invites the pilgrims to the front of the church or worship space; he asks them to face the assembly and invites the assembly to extend their hands in blessing while he prays:

Loving God, throughout our history we have experienced your presence with your people as they journeyed together in pilgrimage to the kingdom proclaimed by your Son. Be with these young pilgrims and guide their way according to your will. Shelter them by day and night from all that might harm them. May they travel in safety, arrive in peace, and return to us in joy. May they continue to experience the fullness of love in your Son, Jesus, through whom we make our prayers.

All: Amen.

Here it may be appropriate to give the pilgrims a medal, the world youth day pin, a cross, or some other memento from the parish/diocesan community in celebration of their undertaking the pilgrimage and as a pledge of the community's prayers while they are away.

It would also be appropriate for a young person to respond in thanksgiving to the community, speaking of the meaning of the pilgrimage for the group, asking for prayers while they are gone, and promising prayers for those friends and family who remain behind.

Concluding Prayer:
Presider:

May the Lord guide you and direct your journey in safety.

All: Amen.

Presider:
May the Lord be your companion along the way.

All: Amen.

Presider:
May the Lord grant that the journey you now undertake in faith and hope be marked by loving service to your companions on the journey, and may you experience the constant loving protection of God.

All: Amen.

These concluding prayers adapted from the Book of Blessings, *p. 213.*

Closing Song:
The pilgrims process out with the presider to receive the individual greetings of the assembly.

· · · · ·

PRAYER SERVICE

(To support those on pilgrimage)

By Ms. Leota Roesch
Archdiocese of San Antoino
Director of Training and Formation

This prayer service could be used by the parish in general or by a group of parents whose sons and daughters are on pilgrimage. It could easily be incorporated into a renewal gathering, a neighborhood home liturgy, etc.

Opening/Gathering Prayer
Proclamation of the Word: John 10:7-10

Response:
Parents, family members, friends, parish staff, and others are invited to share with those assembled what they have heard from specific young people in Denver. How have they experienced "fullness of life" while on pilgrimage?

Intercessions:
The Lord is near to those who call on him. May God protect our sons and daughters so that they will experience the fullness of life promised to them, we pray. . . .
Wherever life leads these young people, may they find that God is with them on all of life's journeys to protect and guide them, we pray. . . .
As Mary our Mother released her son that he might do the will of His Father, may we let go of our sons and daughters that they may find and do the will of God, we pray. . . .
May we support these young people in their

searching, in their questioning, and in their growing, we pray. . . .
(Other intercessions are offered as are particular to the gathered assembly.)

Prayer Leader:
May God remain constantly at our side and with our young people on pilgrimage and mercifully guide all of our journeys in ways that are pleasing and just. We make our prayer through Jesus Christ Our Lord.

All: Amen.

Support Action:
Pen, papers, and envelopes are provided for all the assembly. They are asked to write a letter of support to a young person they might know (or to their son/daughter) who is on the pilgrimage (or to the group of young people in general). The letter could include an ongoing promise of prayer; a statement of how the person has taught the letter writer about living a life of faith; what the letter writer hopes for the future of the young person; etc. The letter writer is asked to deliver the letter to the young pilgrim when he/she returns. Letters to the group in general can be delivered to the parish office. Instrumental music can be played while the people are writing.

Sign of Peace

Closing Prayer:
Good and gracious God, we recall your presence with Abraham and Sarah and their family as they departed from their own people to the land you gave them, with the nation of Israel in their wandering and in the Promised Land, with the Magi whom you guided to the Christ, with the Holy Family as they fled to Egypt, and with us in all of our journeying. Continue to protect all of us and be with our sons and daughters especially, walk by their side, be their companion on their pilgrimage, enliven them with your Spirit, and return them to us safely. We ask this in the name of your Son, our brother, Jesus. Amen.

Prayer Leader:
May almighty God bless us, hear our prayers for our children, and be with us and them in our life's journey.

All: Amen.

Prayer Leader:
And may almighty God bless us, the Father, and the Son, + and the Holy Spirit.

All: Amen.

· · · · ·

WELCOMING PILGRIMS ON THEIR RETURN

(To be integrated into the first Sunday's liturgy after the youths' return from Denver. We suggest Sunday, August 22nd.)

Suggested Gathering Song for the Liturgy:

World Youth Day song or Marty Haugen, "Bring Forth the Kingdom," Copyright © 1986, 7404 S. Mason Ave. Chicago, Ill., 60638, It would be appropriate for the pilgrims to enter the church in procession with the ministers for the liturgy. The presider may wish briefly to acknowledge the young people at the beginning of the Introductory Rite.

General Intercessions:

We know that we have no lasting city here on earth. May we always be pilgrims seeking the Heavenly Jerusalem, let us pray. . . .

We have learned to recognize the signs of God's presence with us in our life's journey. May we come to recognize Jesus as our companion on that journey and may we know him in the breaking of the bread, let us pray. . . .

We are grateful for the Lord's care of us on our pilgrimage. May we always be hospitable to the strangers God sends into our lives, let us pray. . . .

We are also grateful for the support of our parents, family, and friends. May we support them in their pilgrimage here on earth and may we all come together to our heavenly home, let us pray. . . .

(These intercessions are in addition to the other petitions offered by the community.)

After Communion, a young person representing the group who went to Denver addresses the assembly, sharing with them the graces given by God during the pilgrimage, describing some of the high points of the experience (in terms of experiencing "life to the fullest" as opposed to merely describing the events), and thanking the assembly for its support and prayers.

Prayer of Blessing:

Before the Dismissal Rite, the presider invites the pilgrims to come before the community and face them. He invites the community assembled to extend their hands in blessing as he prays:

Glory and praise be to you, God, who gives us fullness of life through your son and our brother, Jesus. These young people have chosen to follow you and are eager to continue in their faith. They generously embrace your command "to go out to whole world" and willingly they tell of your goodness. We ask you to bless them, so that their lives might be for us a reminder of wondrous deeds and everlasting love. We ask this through Christ our Lord.

All: Amen.

Prayers over the People:
(Adapted from the Book of Blessings, *p. 218)*

Presider:

May God, the Lord of heaven and earth, who so graciously has accompanied you on this pilgrimage, continue to protect you.

All: Amen.

Presider:

May God, who has gathered all of us in Christ Jesus, grant that you will be of one heart and one mind in Christ.

All: Amen.

Presider:

May God, whose goodness inspires in you all that you desire and achieve, strengthen your devotion and bless you.

All: Amen.

. . . . .

RECONCILIATION

RECONCILIATION AND HEALING

By John W. Crossin, OSFS
and Sheila Garcia

War, ethnic fighting, racial strife, domestic violence, bitter divorce — few young people today can escape the conflicts that surround them. Even if not directly involved in these situations, young people know that our world cries out for healing and reconciliation. But they also experience this need for healing as a personal one. Confronted by the inevitable conflict and pain involved in growing up and entering adulthood, young people seek healing and the peace of heart that comes with it.

Healing in our Church is a multifaceted reality that comes in a variety of ways. Many have been healed in reading Scripture: we know that God has spoken to us and we are healed. Healing also takes place in prayer, when we can experience a deep reconciliation with God and neighbor. The Eucharist, the central prayer of the Catholic community, is a sign of God's great love for us and a celebration of ongoing healing and reconciliation. It is a time of closeness to God when we focus on God's presence and let it transform us. Through Christ's power the ravages of sin can be transformed as we ask for forgiveness. If we can get beyond our familiarity (not always easy) we can be deeply touched by the power of the Spirit evident here. Thus we can be energized to be a healing presence to reach out to others in the wider community.

Within the Catholic community, the Sacrament of Reconciliation is a primary means of healing. It is a sacrament worthy of serious preparation, one that can be a powerful, spiritual experience with profound effects. Like the other sacraments, reconciliation is a gift from God in which we personally encounter the Giver. Each time we approach reconciliation, then, we open ourselves to encountering Jesus in a deeply personal way. Since relationships are so important to young people, it is essential that they experience this sacrament as a personal call from Jesus to share His life.

Sacramental reconciliation is very much related to a person's sense of sin. We all need this sacrament, since we are all sinners. God has called us to be in relationship with him and with each other. That means opening ourselves up both to give and to receive love. Yet we know that we have often failed to grow in love in our relationships: we have sinned. When discussing the sacrament with young people we need to put it in the context of the young person's relationship with God and neighbor.

As we embark on this pilgrimage to Denver for World Youth Day, we are invited to reflect on our relationship with God and with each other. Guided by the Holy Spirit and encouraged by the prayers and example of our fellow pilgrims, we are invited to examine our lives, to acknowledge those places where we have failed to grow in love of God and neighbor, and to ask forgiveness. Then, in Denver, we are invited to join in a reconciliation service with the Holy Father and thousands of young people from around the world, as a powerful sign of God's healing power that unites our human family.

Today we are learning to look more closely at the roots of personal sin. We have moved from just looking at lists and numbers of sins to seeking the causes of sin. Here young people can be guided to look at the underlying patterns of their lives and activity which lead to sin. By learning to look at the causes of sinful activity young people grow towards Christian maturity.

The power of the Lord in this sacrament can heal the deepest roots and fissures of sin and give ongoing strength and power for the journey. Here is a time to confess and let go of the results of sin. Our sins have their impact on ourselves and others. Perhaps the persons whom we have hurt have disappeared from our lives, and we never hear from them again. The sacrament provides an opportunity to turn people and past events over to the Lord, realizing that his love can bring good out of evil.

The sacrament brings us face-to-face with the reality that we are not perfect and never will be. We are pilgrims and will always have our struggles. The sacrament, especially in its face-to-face format, provides an occasion to share a bit of one's life story and to ask a few questions. For young people, this can be an important (and perhaps rare opportunity to share or to ask important questions.

Finally, we can help young people appreciate the value of sacramental reconciliation by connecting it to events in their everyday lives. How have young people already experienced healing and forgiveness in their relationships with parents, siblings, or friends? How have they learned to say "I'm sorry" and, in turn, accepted the "I'm sorry" of another? We can help young people reflect on these experiences and connect them to the healing and forgiveness that Jesus offers us in the sacrament.

But we also need to realize that young people are future-oriented. Reconciliation looks not just to the past, but to the future. In the sacrament God gives us the grace to do things we could never do on our own. Having experienced the gift of God's forgiveness, we now go out to share the gift of reconciliation with others: by mending the personal relationships that sin has weakened and, equally challenging, working for reconciliation in the larger society. Jesus has given us our mission when he proclaimed "Blessed are the peacemakers." That peace, beginning in our own hearts, becomes a gift that young people share with the world.

· · · · ·

IDEAS FOR RECONCILIATION WITH ADOLESCENTS

From *Adolescent Spirituality* by Rev. Charles Shelton SJ

(Reprinted with permission.)

1. Because the "group" is a pivotal influence in the adolescent years, it is often advantageous to present reconciliation in a group setting. For example, the sacrament might be administered within the setting of an athletic team, a school class, a retreat group, a social club, or a dormitory floor. This approach is often a supportive experience.

2. Because relationships are a major concern for adolescents, discussions of this sacrament should be placed in the context of the young person's relationship with God and neighbor. Focus on sin as rela-

tional and stress this aspect in all discussions of this sacrament.

3. When adolescents do realize personal transgressions, stress the healing and forgiving aspects of the sacrament. At the same time, however, the significance of this sacrament should not be limited to this healing and forgiving experience. Rather, discuss the sacrament in terms of where this experience now leads the adolescent. What conversion might follow from this experience? What growth might take place? How does this sacramental reception aid the adolescent on the road to Christian maturity? The thrust of this sacrament must have a definite future orientation.

4. Discuss this sacrament in the context of the values it represents. We have already stressed the fundamental importance of values in the adolescent's moral growth. Explore the adolescent's own experiences of forgiveness and healing. How important are these events in the adolescent's life? Likewise, how does the adolescent show forgiveness and healing to others? Does he or she place any priority on showing forgiveness and healing to others?

5. Discuss together with the adolescent and reflect on the deep bond between this sacrament and the life of Jesus. Because relational demands and needs are so strong in adolescence, they emphasize Jesus as healer, friend, and reconciler. It is essential that adolescents experience this sacrament as a personal call from Jesus to share his life, despite our own personal weaknesses (2 Cor 12:10).

6. Regardless of what dialog might take place, adolescents will often exhibit alienation from this sacrament. In a pastoral context, it is best to minister to the individual needs of the adolescent. In dialog with each adolescent, we must emphasize our own acceptance of the adolescent and help him or her to grow in personal reflection and self-insight.

· · · · ·

COMMUNITY SERVICE AND CATHOLIC SOCIAL TEACHING

IN SERVICE OF CHRIST'S ABUNDANT LIFE

The life Jesus brings is deeply spiritual and profoundly social. It is rooted in the Creator, the source of all life. It is redeemed by Jesus, who conquered death with new life. And it is shaped by the Spirit who calls us to renew the earth.

To be in service of Christ's abundant life, we must first be willing to stand for the dignity and rights of the human person. We stand for a just and compassionate society where we measure our progress by how far "the least of these" are faring. We stand for a world where injustice and violence give way to healing and reconciliation. Believers are called to choose life, defend life, protect life, and to insist on the fullness of life for all God's children. This is a huge task in a nation where 1.6 million children are destroyed before birth, in a society where 30 million lack access to health care, in a world where 40 thousand children die every day from hunger and its consequences.

To be in service of Christ's abundant life we must first be open to standing in solidarity with the entire family of God in all its national, racial, economic, religious, and political diversity. Our first service to the world is to love our neighbor, recognizing that every person is our neighbor. Service is most meaningful when the person who serves understands who is being served and why they need assistance.

In this year of preparation for World Youth Day, all young adults and youth are called to participate in service to our neighbors. Let the service we do reflect the abundant life that Jesus has opened to us. Some possibilities include:

Set up and run a Vacation Bible School for children in shelter programs or schools for the mentally or emotionally disabled.

Sponsor a community education program on AIDS at shopping centers.

Get a "wish list" from a shelter program and sponsor a drive for "hard to get" items such as new underwear and socks.

Invite the volunteer coordinators from community service agencies to a Service Fair for your school or parish where volunteers can shop for types of service they can offer.

Participate or sponsor a workcamp to improve the quality of housing. Habitat for Humanity is a good contact!

Host an Easter Egg Hunt/Prayer Service for your parish and encourage families to attend.

Compile and print a list of resources for families. Include information about crisis services, counseling, health care, family based entertainment, books, family prayer, and more.

Work at a soup kitchen, volunteer to provide a meal at a shelter, or deliver sandwiches to homeless on the street.

Designate 10 percent of money made in fund raisers to a specific charity.

Visit the elderly, nursing homes, children's wards at local hospitals at times other than Christmas. Schedule a St. Patrick's Day sing-a-long or a puppet show for no special reason at all.

Service opportunities that put us in touch with those who stand to benefit from the service are always the best. Service opportunities that allow us to work together with our peers are also preferred but not always possible. If you have young adults or youth who are engaged in several different types of service where they are not working together, maybe you could set up evenings of prayer and discussion. These evenings could be helpful in supporting those who serve. Also think about keeping the work of those who serve before the community. The school newspaper, parents' newsletters, or parish bulletins are good places to share the good news of service.

. . . . . .

RESOURCES ON CATHOLIC SOCIAL TEACHING

By Nancy Wisdo
Associate Director
Department of Social Development and World Peace

"I came so that they may have life and have it more abundantly." (Jn 10:10)

The following resources are offered to youth, young adult, and campus ministers to help them integrate the values and principles of Catholic social teaching into their work especially during this year of preparation for World Youth Day. The theme, taken from Jn 10:10, speaks of a fullness of life for all of God's children. Unfortunately, we see all around us evidence that abundant life — economic, physical, and spiritual — is denied to many in our society and our world because of social ills such as racism, abortion, poverty, and war.

In these critical times, the basic principles of our social tradition: the dignity of every person, the option for the poor, solidarity with the global community can be a source of hope and a challenge to young people. Sharing and acting on the teaching is a work of faith and an act of love. It helps bring down the barriers that keep all of us from living life abundantly.

The following resources are available from the U.S. Catholic Conference through the Department of Social Development and World Peace and the Campaign for Human Development:

Videos

I Am Only A Child: compelling reflection on the state of our children in our nation and our world. Can be used in conjunction with the Catholic Campaign for Children and the bishops' statement, *Putting Children and Families First.* VHS, 14 minutes, $24.95. Available from: Lumen Catechetical Consultants, Inc., P.O. Box 1761, Silver Spring, Md. 20915

Bring Down the Walls: produced for the 100th anniversary of *Rerum Novarum.* Provides an introduction to the basic principles of Catholic social teaching and some examples of the Church's efforts to share and act on the teaching to influence public policy. VHS, 14 minutes, $19.91. Available from: Lumen Catechetical Consultants

Sisters and Brothers Among Us: tells the story of poverty through the faces and voices of the poor. Produced by the Diocese of Joliet. VHS, 16 minutes,

$9.00. Available from: Campaign for Human Development, 3211 Fourth St., N.E., Washington, D.C. 20017.

Marketplace Prophets: Voices for Justice in the 20th Century: documentary on Catholic social teaching, produced by NBC-TV; is a review of the Catholic Church's commitment to justice. It highlights the work of CHD and Catholic Charities USA. VHS, 60 minutes, $29.95. Available from: Office for Publishing and Promotion Services, United States Catholic Conference, Video No. 427-9. Call 1-800-235-8722 to order.

Written Materials

Putting Children and Families First: A Challenge for Our Church, Nation, and World: examines the needs of all children in an increasingly difficult world. Presents the moral and religious dimensions of caring for children. No. 469-4, 24 pp. Bulk discounts.

Political Responsibility: Revitalizing American Democracy: focuses on the individual Catholic's role as a responsible citizen and voter. Includes the Church's position on major issues of public policy. No. 467-8, 40 pp., English/Spanish. Bulk discounts.

Communities of Hope, Parishes and Substance Abuse: A Practical Guide: a companion document to the pastoral statement on substance abuse, New Slavery, New Freedom, which is included in this printing. No. 473-2, 24 pp. Bulk discounts.

Renewing the Earth: An Invitation to Reflection and Action on Environment in Light of Catholic Social Teaching: the United States bishops' contribution to the debate on ecology and environment. No. 468-6, 14 pp. Bulk discounts.

A Century of Social Teaching: A Common Heritage, A Continuing Challenge: a brief, popular look at Catholic social teaching written for the anniversary of Rerum Novarum. No. 379-5, 16 pp. Bulk discounts.

To order these written materials and additional documents including the pastoral letters on war and peace and on the economy, contact: Office for Publishing and Promotion Services, United States Catholic Conference, 3211 Fourth St. N.E., Washington, D.C. 20017 or call 1-800-235-8722.

· · · · ·

PRAYER TO CELEBRATE SERVICE TO GOD'S PEOPLE

Becoming "Yes"
Youth Energized through Service

By Marilyn Haggerty
Diocese of Brownsville
Office of Youth Ministry

Before the Prayer Service

Cut out articles on current world problems or issues from newspapers (e.g., war, drugs, election, AIDS, family issues, addiction). Tape or paste them onto white or colored typing paper which has the song "Here I Am, Lord" or " Digo Sí, Señor" printed on the other side. Prepare enough for the expected number at the prayer service.

Prepare a list of all the service opportunities in which the youth or young adults participated during the last year.

In the prayer service room, put a world map (or large picture of the world) on one wall and light it with a lamp or overhead projector. Just before the prayer service, tape the newspaper articles on the world picture or map and darken the room, except for the world map or picture.

1. Gathering

The participants gather in another room and come into the prayer room while the song "From a Distance" (Bette Midler) or "Place in This World" (Michael W. Smith) plays. They sit facing the map or world picture.

2. Introduction
Leader:

God calls each of us Christians to reach out to others in our world through service. Jesus' life and the stories he told give us examples of how we can connect our faith with real issues. As young people, we can make a difference in today's world. So we gather today to celebrate what we have already done and to discover new ways to serve others, God, and our world.

Líder: Dios nos llama como cristianos para que lleguemos a otras personas por medio del servicio. La vida de Jesucristo y las historias que Él contó nos ofrecen ejemplos de cómo poder relacionar nuestra fe con los eventos de la vida real. Como gente joven, ustedes pueden causar la diferencia en el mundo de hoy. Nos reunimos hoy para celebrar lo que hemos hecho y para descubrir nuevas formas de servir a otros, a Dios y a nuestro mundo.

3. Opening Prayer
Leader:

Creator God, be present with us at this time. We know that you created our world and we thank you for all the good things of the earth. Show us how to care for the earth and all the people and animals living on it. Give us courage to speak up in a crowd when we have gifts to share. Help us to be unafraid about what others will say about us and to stand up and follow the example of your Son, Jesus Christ. Keep alive in our mind and heart the desire for a better world, and help us to be able truly to say, "Yes, I can make a difference." We ask this through Christ our Lord. Amen.

Líder: Dios, creador, ven a estar con nosotros en este momento. Sabemos que tú creaste nuestro mundo y te damos gracias por todas las cosas buenas que hay. Enséñanos a preocuparnos por este mundo, por la gente y por los animales que viven en él. Danos valor para compartir nuestras ideas y sentimientos en los grupos en que participamos. Ayúdanos a no temer lo que la gente diga de nosotros y danos valor para enfrentarnos a la vida y seguir el ejemplo de tu Hijo Jesucristo. Mantén vivo en nuestra mente y corazón el deseo por un mundo mejor y ayúdanos a poder decir, "Sí, yo puedo causar la diferencia."

4. Scripture Reading/ Enactment
Options:

1. Feeding the 4000 (Mt 15:29-39; Mk 8:1-9)
2. Good Samaritan (Lk 10:29-37)
3. The Last Judgement (Mt 25:31-46)

The passage may be enacted (in original or modern settings) or the participants may be asked to close their eyes and imagine they are one of the characters in the story as it is read slowly.

5. Reflection

Choose several young adults or youth to reflect on what happened in the story. What did Jesus ask of his followers? With what characters did the young people identify? What does the story say about service today and in the lives of the young people?

6. Prayer for the World's Needs

Ask each participant to remove one article from the map and to sit down. Explain that these are articles from the newspaper about problems in the world. Just as the people in the Scripture were called to respond to the needs of the people of the world, so we are each called to make a difference in our world both through prayer and action.

Ask each young person to read the short article (or underlined portion of the article) and to pray silently about the problem or issue covered in the article. Soft instrumental music may be played in the background. As a prayer of petition, ask volunteers to name their issue by saying: For the _____ We pray to the Lord. Everyone responds with: Lord, hear our prayer.

7. Prayer of Service: Naming What We Have Already Done
Leader:

As Christians, we are called to bring hope to our world through service to one another. Our world needs both you and me to put the stories and words of Jesus into action. What we do may seem like a small act in a world with big problems, but if each of us does something, our actions will multiply and our world will change. We will make a difference. During this year (or last year), we were involved in many ways of serving others. We would like to celebrate these by naming them and having those who participated stand up and remain standing. Please join in and sing the chorus of "Here I Am, Lord" (or "Digo Sí, Señor") every time the song leader begins. The words are on the back of the newspaper article.

Líder: Como cristianos somos llamados a traer esperanza a nuestro mundo por medio del servicio de unos a otros. Nuestro mundo nos necesita para poner las historias y las palabras de Jesús en acción. Lo que nosotros hagamos tal vez se verá como un acto pequeño en un mundo con problemas grandes, pero si cada uno hace algo, nuestras acciones se multiplicarán y nuestro mundo cambiará. Nosotros actuaremos y nuestro mundo cambiará. Nosotros causaremos la diferencia. Durante este año (o el año pasado), participamos en diferentes formas de servir a otros. Nos gustaría honrar a estas personas nombrando a cada una. Pónganse de pié y permanezcan así. Todos juntos cantemos el coro Digo Sí, Señor cuando el líder del coro empiece.

The leader starts singing the first verse of "Here I Am, Lord" or "Digo Sí, Señor." When she or he gets to the chorus, the young people are invited to join in. After the chorus, three or four service activities are read from the list of service opportunities. The leader of the prayer service leads into the chorus of the song by saying: The youth who were involved in these service activities answered God's call to serve the poor and those who may be considered outcasts in society. When Jesus calls on you to serve others, what will you say? The song leader then leads into the chorus of the song. After each chorus, three or four more service activities are read from the list and the leader leads the gathering back to the chorus using the following:

Los jóvenes que participaron en las actividades de servicio han contestado la llamada de Dios a servir a los pobres y a los que la sociedad considera inútiles. Cuando Jesús te llame para servir a otros, ¿qué le dirás?

These young people have heard God's call too and they are taking action to help build up their parish and civic community. When Jesus calls on you to serve others, what will you say?

Estos jóvenes también han oido la llamada de Dios y estan actuando para ayudar a su parroquia y a su comunidad a crecer. Cuando Jesús te llame para servir a otros, ¿qué le dirás?

These young people have found that they can touch the lives of others in very real ways. What are you doing in your parish? What are the needs you see? When Jesus calls on you to serve others, what will you say?

Estos jóvenes se han dado cuenta que pueden afectar las vidas de otros en diferentes maneras. ¿Qué estás haciendo en nuestra parroquia ¿Qué necesidades ves tú? Cuando Jesús te llame para servir a otros, ¿qué le dirás?

After the last group of service activities is named, ask everyone else to stand as a sign for their own commitment to serve. Sing the chorus twice.

8. Commitment to Service in the Future
The leader of the prayer service invites each young person to write down one act of service they would be willing to commit to do during the next month (e.g., help serve a meal at the shelter for the homeless, write a short letter to a legislator about the U.N. Convention on the Rights of the Child, help in the cleanup of a local neighborhood park) and then to place the paper back on the world map or picture with their service commitment showing. A song such as "We Are the World" may be played during this time.

9. Closing Prayer
Conclude with a short closing prayer.

· · · · ·

FAMILY INVOLVEMENT AND FOLLOW-UP ACTIVITIES

ON THE WAY TO DENVER, DON'T FORGET THE FAMILY!

Richard McCord
Associate Director
Secretariat for Women, Family, Laity, and Youth

We start our life's journey in a family and, along the way, we return to it, either physically or spiritually, either to repeat the lessons we learned there or to react against what we endured. As someone once put it, "The family is the primary lens that filters the early and lasting light of every life."

In addition to their peer group, the family is a most important community in the lives of young people. The family's power to form, to transform, and sometimes to deform, is unique and primary. Even as they begin or continue the developmental process of separating themselves from it, young people still look to their families not only for roots, but also for wings.

Ordinary family life contains within it moments of great significance for the development of every person and for the vitality of the whole Church. While family life reveals unresolved tensions and even creates its own kind of stress, it also provides stability and support in a world often lacking these qualities. Families offer an immediate context for establishing and testing Christian love. Families engender the values and teach the skills that are so necessary to the process of becoming Christ's disciples.

Families are an essential part of the celebration of World Youth Day 1993. It is they who have been shaping for many years the young people who will journey to Denver. It is they who will welcome the pilgrims home from Denver. In some cases, too, they will be able to share the actual experience of this International Meeting in Denver with their sons and daughters, their sisters and brothers. World Youth Day 1993 is, even without our planning it, a family event. But there are steps we can take to make its value more explicit both for young people and their families. Part of our challenge in this preparation period is to maintain a family perspective.

When something, especially a once-in-a-lifetime experience, happens to one member of a family, it will inevitably affect the rest of the family in positive and negative ways. World Youth Day 1993 is a good example. If for this reason only, it would benefit

(Denver Metro & Convention Bureau)

parents and other family members to prepare for World Youth Day in their home and family settings.

But there is another reason for families to be involved in the celebration of World Youth Day. World Youth Day is an invitation to the whole Church, an effort of the entire ecclesial community. Christian families are, in a real yet unique way, an embodiment of the Church. They are, in the words of the Second Vatican Council (*Lumen Gentium,* 11), a "domestic church." Pope Paul VI expanded this seminal teaching when he declared:

This means that there should be found in every Christian family the various aspects of the entire Church. . . . [T]he family, like the Church, ought to be a place where the Gospel is transmitted and from which the Gospel radiates (*Evangelii Nuntiandi,* 71).

And Pope John Paul II has continued to develop this teaching and to remind us how central family life is to the life and mission of the Church. In Familiaris Consortio (70) he writes: "No plan for organized pastoral ministry at any level must ever fail to take into consideration. . . the family."

These words should echo throughout our preparation for World Youth Day as a reminder of the formative role of a family, as an invitation to value its life and tasks, and as a challenge to see families as true partners in ministry with parishes, schools, youth groups, and other church structures.

Without the "home church" the whole Church is incomplete. So, on the way to Denver, let's not forget the family!

· · · · ·

IDEAS FOR FAMILIES FOR THE YEAR OF PREPARATION 1993

By Carol Pacione
Coordinator of Family Ministry
Archdiocese of Baltimore

> "I came so that they might have life, and
> have it more abundantly."
>
> John 10:10

Throughout this Year of Preparation for the visit of Pope John Paul II, families are encouraged to share prayer, discussion, celebrations, and service and to become evangelizers among their peers. We are called to mark this year by giving to one another the love that Jesus has bestowed upon us. To live in Christ is to live abundantly. The following may provide for families with adolescents and/or young adults ideas on which to build a more loving, life-giving relationship between family members and a stronger partnership between families and the larger community.

Families with Adolescents

Family Meal Time. Once a traditional gathering time for family members, meal times have been reduced to merry-go-round nutrition because of all of the meetings, activities, and schedule demands on families. During this Year of Preparation, try at least once a week to eat together; to "catch up" on each others lives, to share, and to discuss. Perhaps part of the meal discussion could center on the news reporting of World Youth Day and the papal visit. Prayers of thanksgiving for the abundance in our lives and a petition to help us see more clearly how to share this abundance — emotional security as well as physical comforts — could be part of the meal time prayer.

Simple Meals. As we reflect on all that has been given to us by God, let us ask ourselves what are the implications for our family as part of a larger national and international family? Once a month share a simple meal of soup, bread, and raw vegetables. Try not to use electricity in the preparation of this meal and do not allow any snacking later in the evening. Pray for those of our global family who live in poverty and without many of the conveniences we take for granted. How does their simplified life style more closely reflect the life of Jesus?

Sharing Wealth. Jesus came to give abundant life to all. We as his followers are called to share what we have with others. This year is a perfect opportunity to support a child/teen in another country through organizations such as Catholic Relief Services, Compassion International, and Save the Children.

Workcamp Vacation. Many youth and young adults will be journeying to Denver in August. Another pilgrimage which could be enjoyed by entire families would be a workcamp experience. Travel to the city, county, or mountains to work with people who are less fortunate in material possessions but perhaps richer in culture and tradition. By partaking of the lives and lifestyles of others, our faith will be enriched.

Families with Young Adults

Talk Religion and Politics. This is family, not business acquaintances or the neighborhood cocktail party. These subjects should not be taboo, but should stimulate respectful discussion, stretch and challenge thinking, and be a source of faith growth for parents and their young adult children. How do we participate in the abundant life of Jesus in our political decisions? Work ethics? Faith practices? Reactions to and actions about social justice issues?

Support for Young Adults in Transition. The young adult years can be times of stress and struggle, but also a potent opportunity for parents to be witnesses of Jesus' abundant love. Some of the times when our support may be most needed included: entering and graduating from college, wrestling with career choices and searching for employment, struggles with faith and religious practices, engagement for marriage or the "break-up" of a serious relationship. Subtle support through phone calls, letters, and an empathic ear will demonstrate to our children the unconditional love that Jesus invites us to share.

Resource for Family Prayer: In addition to the suggested prayers for families preparing for the pilgrimage to Denver, see *Catholic Household Blessings and Prayers,* USCC, 1989. "Blessing before Leaving on a Journey," p. 284; "Blessing upon Returning from a Journey, " p. 289.

· · · · ·

BRINGING THE STORY HOME

Affirmations for Black Family Ministry

By Nathan Jones PhD. © 1992
Reprinted from Making It Plain
With permission of David C. Cook Publishing Company

> "Where two or three are gathered in my name, there am I in their midst."
>
> Mt 18:20

For the first three centuries, Christians did not gather to worship in churches but rather in their own homes. The home became a place of hospitality and worship. The disciples of Jesus were sent in twos to the households of Israel to preach and to receive hospitality from the table of welcoming families. And Paul, the travelling preacher, visited various cities and made households his meeting places.

Christian faith, therefore, has its origins in simple gatherings of family and friends in the rhythm of ordinary life. Daily experiences of care, support, forgiveness, and affirmation help us to discover in a "down home" way what God's love is really all about.

African American families today are under considerable stress. These stresses present severe strains on meaningful relationships, stable marriages, and effective child-rearing while tearing at the foundation of healthy family life. No single aspect of Black life is in need of more serious attention by the churches than the family.

The Church has the weighty challenge to assist the family in deepening its own bonding and planning its own ministry. Here are several affirmations to guide your local planning.

1. Let there be family. Affirm the existence of loving relationships among Black people. The size or shape of the family doesn't matter as much as the spirit and quality of interpersonal relationships. Since parenting cannot be taken lightly, invite households to formally dedicate themselves to living a deeper Christian life together.

2. Let there be a plan. We often fail because we fail to plan. What is necessary to improve the quality of our relationships and secure the future of our children? Establish high, yet realistic, expectations of one another. Low expectations produce low achievers; high expectations produce high achievers. What agreements and understandings are critical to achieve for a more satisfying family life?

3. Let there be affirmation. We must recognize the strengths and goodness in each other. The willingness to express acceptance and belonging goes a long way to secure the identity and self-worth of family members. Respect for authority is not increased by spankings, "put downs, " lecturing or loud talk. Difficulties arise when we devalue ourselves and others.

4. Let there be freedom. Being seen and not heard. Adhering to the spoken word of adults without question. These are strict, oppressive and parent-controlled child-rearing attitudes that are familiar to us. Encourage adults to model behavior they wish children would emulate. Making mistakes is acceptable in order to learn to appreciate the consequences of one's behavior. We need family roots but we also need wings!

5. Let there be memories. Each family has memories of God's influence. Promote a conscious attempt to keep family traditions and customs alive or create new ones. Today many children feel cut off from their past. Family meetings allow time for decisions affecting the whole family to be made jointly. In a household of faith, every activity carries a religious meaning.

6. Let there be love. Family members should accept each other unconditionally but love enough to invite one another to grow. The family as a "household of faith" radiates the Good News in its everyday life, its activities, struggles, and prayer. We supply for one another the nourishment and support that are seldom received outside. Family nourishes the capacity of its members to express a living faith through action in the world.

· · · · ·

BEYOND THE GATHERING

The pilgrimage is over. The crowds have left. You are home and although the songs from Denver still echo in your head, you know that the World Youth Day Gathering has ended. So what do you do now? Here are some ideas that might help you after you return from Denver. Here are some ideas to help you put closure on the experience and to help you let that experience impact your community.

1. Schedule a debriefing meeting. Gather the pilgrims to reflect on the experience. Take time to talk with other pilgrims about what you felt and saw. Begin to identify the ideas that you want to bring home. Make plans to give the ideas that you have gathered to the right people in your school or parish.

2. Let your story be heard. Ask young people to share their experience with the larger community at a school assembly or weekend liturgy. Write personal reflections on the WYD experience and print them in parish or school newsletters. Set up meetings with local press and media to help them generate follow-up coverage.

3. Host a Family Event. Have a pot luck dinner for families of those who journeyed to Denver. Share pictures and slides. Take time to pray for a successful pilgrimage and safe passage.

4. Bring Gifts. Plan ahead to bring a gift back to your family, parish, or school community. Gifts might include a picture to be framed or a new song to learn and sing, a prayer card, or a piece of art. A gift can help the community share in the experience. (Maybe you could share gifts with your hosts at the hub cities as you return home.)

5. Retreat Day/Evening of Reflection. Carry the message and the learning of World Youth Day back to your parish or school by hosting an evening for reflection and discussion or a retreat day. (Bringing the Story Home, in this resource manual on page 00.)

6. Keep It Going. Continue to do the service and the evangelization that was begun in preparation for World Youth Day. Can the community accept the challenge to continue the service for a year? Has the outreach and evangelization brought new members to the community? Will they be considering the RCIA?

7. Continued Service. Having participated in World Youth Day with the Holy Father, bishops, priests, deacons, religious, and lay ministers, consider the possibility of continued service to the Church in priesthood or religious life. Diocesan and religious vocation ministers could follow-up on the Denver experience by offering opportunities for vocation discernment among those who participated. Dioceses might consider using an established program to invite participants, youth leaders, etc. to surface names of individuals who may demonstrate the potential for ministry and leadership in the life of the Church. Two possibilities are: Called by Name, United States Catholic Conference, Pub. No.183-0, and Operation Andrew, scheduled for publication in the spring of 1993.

8. Connect with Other Events. Carry the energy of the World Youth Day Gathering to other gathering events: diocesan young adult gatherings, diocesan youth rally, National Catholic Youth Conference, National Catholic Student Coalition Leadership Conference.

9. Reflect and Pray. Encourage those who traveled to Denver to take the time to reflect and pray. Here are some possible avenues for your meditation.

What did I learn about myself? my country? my church? the world? How am I different as a result of my journey? What have I learned that was new? How am I the same? What did I already know that was affirmed?

Where did I see God in my travels? What was God's message to me?

Will my experience at WYD lead me to do anything new or different in my life? Did my experience give me ideas that I would like to use in our parish or school community? Will WYD remain a memory or will it lead to follow-up actions? What will they be?

10. Continue the momentum begun for the Denver event. In the parish, school, college develop leadership for ministry among the young adults and youth who were present; strengthen existing programs for young adults, college students and teens, or develop parish or campus programs.

• • • • •

APPENDIX

THE PAPACY

Roman Catholic theology and canon law attribute to the pope a variety of titles. These include Successor of Peter, Head of the Church, Vicar of Christ, Bishop of Rome, Patriarch of the West and Sovereign of the State of Vatican City.

The word *pope* comes from the Latin *papa* which derives from the Greek *pappas,* in classical times a child's word for father. Although originally used of bishops in general, from the sixth century onwards it became progressively restricted in the West to the bishop of Rome. The popular title *Holy Father* reflects the same ancient sense of the spiritual paternity.

The claim of the bishop of Rome to be the successor of the apostle Peter is an ancient one going back to at least the middle of the third century. It received its most authoritative formulation at Vatican I (1869-70), the council that defined papal primacy and infallibility.

The New Testament tells us that Jesus chose from among his followers twelve who were to share in various ways in his mission. After his death and resurrection these twelve and others were known as apostles. They were recognized as possessing special authority in matters of discipline and preaching. Among them Peter had a certain primacy. In subsequent ages the Roman Church came to focus on specific texts as embodying this conviction and expressing its own claims (Cf. Mt 16, 18; Lk 22, 32; Jn 21, 15 ff). Because Peter, along with Paul, preached and died in Rome, succession to his role was seen as falling to the bishop of that city.

The institutional history of western Christianity reveals the growing importance of the papal office. Its development, however, was not unopposed. A countervailing emphasis was placed on bishops, ecumenical councils, and national churches. Tensions arising out of these differing emphases were involved in the separation that grew up between the East and the West as well as in the Protestant Reformation.

Between c. 1850 and 1950 the Catholic Church became more centered on the papacy than ever. Church structure was interpreted in monarchical terms. Roman attitudes in liturgy and theology became the norm almost everywhere. Vatican II (1962-65) represents a turning-point in this regard.

The fact of the Council and relative openness and vitality with which it was carried through marked a rediscovery of the role of bishops in establishing universal policy. The new emphasis became an explicit theme of the Council in its discussion of *collegiality.* To become a bishop meant, beyond local responsibilities, to become a member of a world-wide college which shared with the pope responsibility for the whole Church.

Vatican II did not deny the prerogatives attributed to the pope at Vatican I. It tried to balance them, however, with its stress on bishops and on national churches. Out of this has come a shift in the practice of the papacy. Since the Council, for example, synods or meetings of representative bishops from around the world have become a regular feature of church life. Although their decisions are not legally binding on the pope, they provide important occasions for discussion and consultation among the many national churches which in turn sharpen the Vatican's awareness of the issues and concerns confronting the modern Church.

The emphasis on the national church and on the conciliar or episcopal principle has facilitated the ecumenical dialogue. As the Roman Church rediscovers this side of its heritage, Anglicans, Lutherans, and others have been willing to reconsider a ministry or office that could become the center of a reunited Christian Church. Although this is still in the discussion stage, many non-Roman Catholic Christians already recognize the pope a common spokesman especially in the areas of peace, human rights, and economic disparity.

The papacy is a historical institution whose concrete form is constantly undergoing change. For centuries, for example, the pope exercised authority of a political nature over what were known as the Papal States. Although these were lost in 1870, it was only in 1929 that an agreement was reached with Italy setting up the tiny but independent Vatican City.

The relative ease of contemporary travel and the global nature of the modern media are modifying papal practice. The pope has become a much more visible pastor and preacher than ever before.

Notwithstanding the increased emphasis on bishops and on the local churches, the pope remains, under the Scriptures and the binding decisions of the past, the final authority in the Roman Catholic Church.

Father Dan Donovan
Professor of Theology
St. Michael's College
University of Toronto

POPE JOHN PAUL II
BIOGRAPHICAL SKETCH

Karol Joseph Wojtyla [Voy-tee-wah] was born in Wadowice, Poland on May 18, 1920, to an administrative officer in the Polish army and a former schoolteacher. As a young man, Karol was athletic: he enjoyed playing soccer as goalie and took daredevil swims in a flooded Swaka River. He also was an excellent student and he served as president of his school sodality. Karol developed a love of theater and for a time it was his ambition to study literature and become a professional actor.

During Nazi occupation Karol clandestinely pursued both his studies and his acting while working as a stonecutter to support himself and to hold the work permit he needed to avoid deportation or imprisonment. Karol Wojtyla was active in the UNIA, a Christian democratic underground organization. B'ani B'rith and other authorities have testified that he helped Jews find refuge from the Nazis.

While convalescing from an accident, Karol considered a religious vocation and by 1942 he was studying for the priesthood. Karol Wojtyla was ordained a priest on November 1, 1946.

In 1958 Father Wojtyla was named auxiliary bishop of Krakow and four years later he assumed leadership of the diocese with the title of vicar capitular. He was a visible leader often taking a public stand against communism and government officials. Archbishop Wojtyla attend every session of the Second Vatican Council where he helped write several important documents.

In 1967 Pope Paul VI, elevated him to cardinal. By this time several of his poems and writings had been published including *Easter Vigils and Other Poems.* In 1979, his meditations from a papal retreat he conducted were published, *Sign of Contradiction.*

Cardinal Wojtyla traveled often to speak with Catholics in other lands: Canada, the United States, Latin America, Australia, and three trips to West Germany to reconcile Polish people and their former conquerors.

On October 16, 1978, he was elected to succeed Pope John Paul I. He was the first Polish pope and the first non-Italian since Adrian VI in 1522. He was 58 years old. The new pope continued his travels and in 1981 he visited the United States.

That same year Pope John Paul II suffered severe wounds when he was shot as he entered St. Peter's Square to address a general audience. The pope spent two and a half months hospitalized but he fully recovered from his wounds. Two days after Christmas in 1983, the pope went to the prison and met with his would-be assassin. John Paul has kept their conversation confidential.

The Pope has enjoyed hiking, skiing, backpacking, and kayaking. Young people have an even more special place in his heart. In 1985 he called young people to join him for the first World Youth Day celebration in Rome. Since that time he has continued to speak with young people, encouraging them to live the gospels and reach out in a spirit of evangelization to their peers. Pope John Paul II continues to celebrate World Youth Day every other year. In 1993, the World Youth Day celebration will be in Denver, Colorado.

(CNS)

Resources

Pope John Paul II, Catholic Book Publishing Co, New York, New York, 1979.

John Paul II: Pilgrimage of Faith, Seabury Press, New York, New York.

What Do You Seek Young Pilgrims: John Paul II in Santiago de Compostela, 1989 Pontifical Council for the Laity, Documentation Service N. 22, Vatican City, 1991.

"The Holy Father Speaks to Youth 1980-1985," *The Laity Today,* Vatican City, 1985.

"To the Youth of the World," *Youth Update,* 1985, St. Anthony Messenger Press No. Y1085.

· · · · ·

SCHEDULE AT A GLANCE

World Youth Day 1993
The International Gathering for Young Adults
and Youth
August 11 - 15, 1993
Denver, Colorado

Wednesday, August 11, 1993

8:00 p.m.	Opening Mass and ceremony

Thursday, August 12 & Friday, August 13, 1993

8:00 a.m.	Morning prayer
8:00 - 10:00	Sacrament of Penance
10:00 - 12:00	Catechesis, reflection, and discussion(in language groups)
12:00	Mass (in language groups)
Lunch	
3:00 - 5:00	Thematic Events
	(Workshops, cultural events, community service)
Dinner	
8:00 p.m.	Thursday: Cultural events

Friday: Reconciliation Service

10:30 p.m.	Vigil Prayer

Saturday, August 14, 1993

8:00 a.m.	Liturgy to begin pilgrimages
9:00	Pilgrimage to site of evening vigil and Sunday Mass with catechesis along the routes
Lunch	
Dinner	
8:00 p.m.	Vigil Service with the Holy Father

Sunday, August 15, 1993

8:00 a.m.	Morning Prayer at Mass site
10:00 a.m.	Mass of the Assumption
Conclusion of the international meeting	

Please note: Times for events may change.

Housing and Food

Participants will be housed in hotels, motels, "tent cities," campgrounds, schools/parishes, college dorms, and with host families in the Denver area. The average cost of a hotel is $19.00 per person, per night, based on quad occupancy. Host families are being asked to provide complimentary lodging, breakfast, and box lunch, and transportation to and from the nearest neighborhood/parish shuttle bus site. Shuttle service will operate between downtown Denver and parish "hub" centers. All housing is being coordinated by the Denver Metro Visitors and Convention Bureau (1-303-892-1112).

Inexpensive meals will be readily available in the "core area" of downtown Denver, at fast food restaurants and food courts. A special food court will be set up in Celebration Plaza. Restaurants and hotels have agreed to provide meals at reasonable cost. The colleges, retreat centers, and parishes that are housing participants will also make meals available.

All participants are asked to bring a notebook, Bible, and sleeping bag for camping at the Saturday night vigil.

· · · · ·

WORLD YOUTH DAY
DIOCESAN CONTACTS

Diocese of Agana
John W. Hardin
Cuesta San Ramon
Agana, Guam 96910

Diocese of Albany
Ms. Mary Harrison
40 North Main Ave.
Albany, NY 12203

Diocese of Alexandria
Mrs. Sally Dubroc
P.O. Box 7417
Alexandria, LA 71306

Diocese of Allentown
Rev. Philip Rodgers
900 West Market St.
Orwigsburg, PA 17961

Diocese of Amarillo
Rev. Ken Keller
P.O. Box 5644
Amarillo, TX 79117-5644

Diocese of Altoona
Sr. Charmaine Grilliot
126 A Logan Blvd.
Hollidaysburg, PA 16648

Archdiocese of Anchorage
Ms. Susan K. Adam
225 Cordova St.
Anchorage, AK 99501

Diocese of Arlington
Rev. Charles McCoart
200 N. Glebe Rd. #608
Arlington, VA 22203

Archdiocse of Atlanta
Ms. Kathy Wolf
680 West Peachtree St., NW
Atlanta, GA 30308

Diocese of Austin
Mr. Rodrigo E. Reyna
8000 Centre Park Dr.
Suite 160
Austin, TX 78754

Diocese of Baker
Sr. Catherine Hertel, SSMO
P.O. Box 9250
Bend, OR 97708

Archdiocese of Baltimore
Mr. Mark Pacione
320 Cathedral St.
Baltimore, MD 21201

Diocese of Baton Rouge
Mr. Charles Jumonville
3300 Hundred Oaks Ave.
Baton Rouge, LA 70808

Diocese of Beaumont
Mr. Tommy Chatlosh
P.O. Box 3948
Beaumont, TX 77704

Diocese of Belleville
Ms. Collete Lennett
2620 Lebanon Ave.
Belleville, IL 62221

Diocese of Biloxi
Mr. Bragg Moore
P.O. Box 1189
Biloxi, MS 39533

Diocese of Birmingham
Mrs. Marianne Richardson
P.O. Box 12047
Birmingham, AL 35202

Diocese of Bismarck
Ms. Barb Minczewski
P.O. Box 1137
Bismarck, ND 58502

Diocese of Boise
Ms. Jackie Hopper
303 Federal Way
Boise, ID 83705

Archdiocese of Boston
Rev. William T. Schmidt
2121 Commonwealth Ave.
Brighton, MA 02135

Diocese of Bridgeport
Mrs. Olive Greene
238 Jewett Ave.
Bridgeport, CT 06606-2892

Diocese of Brooklyn
Rev. Michael Carrano
6025 Sixth Ave.
Brooklyn, NY 11220

Diocese of Brownsville
Mr. Felipe C. Salinas
P.O. Box 547
Alamo, TX 78516

Diocese of Buffalo
Rev. Gary Bagley
795 Main St.
Buffalo, NY 14203

Diocese of Burlington
Ms. Patricia King
351 North Ave.
Burlington, VT 05401

Diocese of Camden
Mr. Jeffrey Cordner
1845 Haddon Ave.
Camden, NJ 08101

Diocese of Chalan Kanoa
Sister Mary Brigid Perez
P.O. Box 745
Chalan Kanoa, Saipan 96950

Diocese of Charleston
Beverly Jones
1662 Ingram Rd.
Charleston, SC 29409

Diocese of Charlotte
Mrs. Christine Newnan
1524 E. Morehead St.
Charlotte, NC 28207

Diocese of Cheyenne
Mr. Jim Zierden
623 S. Wolcott
Casper, WY 82601

Archdiocese of Chicago
Rev. John Smyth
1150 N. River Rd.
Des Plaines, IL 60016

Archdiocese of Cincinnati
Mr. Sean Reynolds
100 E. Eight St.
Cincinnati, OH 45202

Diocese of Cleveland
Mr. Terry Flanagan
1027 Superior Ave.
Cleveland, OH 44114

Diocese of Colorado Springs
Mr. Kurt Bartley
29 West Kiowa
Colorado Springs, CO 80903

Diocese of Columbus
Father Paul Enke
P.O. Box 1131
Dublin, OH 43017

Diocese of Corpus Christi
Ms. Rosemarie Kamke, Ph. D.
1200 Lantana
Corpus Christi, TX 78407

Diocese of Covington
Ms. Beth Worland
947 Donaldson Rd.
Erlanger, KY 41018

Diocese of Crookston
Mr. Ray Lagasse
1200 Memorial Dr. #610
Crookston, MN 56716

Diocese of Dallas
Ms. Mary Hofer
P.O. Box 190507
Dallas, TX 75219

Diocese of Davenport
Mr. Lawrence Livingston
2706 Gaines St.
Davenport, IA 52804

Archdiocese of Denver
Mr. James Mauck
200 Josephine St.
Denver, CO 80206

Diocese of Des Moines
Mr. Tim Pfau
P.O. Box 1816
Des Moines, IA 50306

Archdiocese of Detroit
Mr. Ray Lemay
305 Michigan Ave.
Detroit, MI 48226

Diocese of Dodge City
Rev. Jonathan Callison
910 Central Ave.
Dodge City, KS 67801

Archdiocese of Dubuque
Mrs. Char McCoy
P.O. Box 479
Dubuque, IA 52004

Diocese of Duluth
Ms. Janice Kilgore
2830 E. 4th St.
Duluth, MN 55812

Diocese of El Paso
Mr. Billy Funk
499 St. Matthews
El Paso, TX 79907

Diocese of Erie
Dr. David Pastrick
429 E. Grandviewd Blvd.
Erie, PA 16514

Diocese of Evansville
Mr. Rick Etienne
P.O. Box 4169
Evansville, IN 47724

Diocese of Fairbanks
Ms. Barbara Thieme
2501 Airport Way
Fairbanks, AK 99709

Diocese of Fall River
Mr. Chris Tanguay
P.O. Box 547
East Freetown, MA 02717

Diocese of Fargo
Mr. Michael Kirby
P.O. Box 1750
Fargo, ND 58107

Diocese of Fresno
Mr. Jim Grant
1530 North Fresno St.
Fresno, CA 93703

Diocese of Ft. Wayne
Mr. Steven Weigand
P.O. Box 390
Fort Wayne, IN 46805

Diocese of Ft. Worth
Ms. Susan Griffin
800 W. Loop 820 S.
Ft. Worth, TX 76108

Diocese of Gallup
Mrs. Lena Clapper
P.O. Box 1615
Aztec, NM 87410

Diocese of Galveston
Brother Jim Barrette
2403 E. Holcomb Blvd.
Houston, TX 77021

Diocese of Gary
Mr. Frank Zalvinski
9292 Bradway
Merrillville, IN 46410

Diocese of Gaylord
Mr. Semmerling, SCSC
1665 M-32 West
Gaylord, MI 49735

Diocese of Grand Island
Ms. Calderone Stewart
P.O. Box 1721
Grand Island, NE 68801

Diocese of Grand Rapids
Mr. Daniel Pierson
660 Burton St., SE
Grand Rapids, MI 49507

Diocese of Great Falls
Mr. Paul Kaiser
P.O. Box 1399
Great Falls, MT 59403

Diocese of Green Bay
Most Rev. Robert Morneau
P.O. Box 23066
Green Bay, WI 54305

Diocese of Greensburg
Ms. Terri Telepak
723 East Pittsburgh St.
Greensburg, PA 15601

Diocese of Harrisburg
Ms. Lucille Smith
4800 Union Deposit Rd.
Harrisburg, PA 17105

Archdiocese of Hartford
Rev. Michael Motta
650 Willard Ave.
Newington, CT 06111

Diocese of Helena
Mr. Jim Tucker
P.O. Box 1729
Helena, MT 59601

Diocese of Honolulu
Mr. John Rezentes
6301 Pali Hwy.
Kaneohe, HI 96744

Diocese of Houma
Mr. Raymond Simon
P.O. Box 9077
Houma, LA 70361

Archdiocese of Indianapolis
Ms. Julie Szolek
1400 N. Meridian St.
Indianapolis, IN 46202

Diocese of Jackson
Mr. Larry Campbell
2225 Boling St.
Jackson, MS 39213

Diocese of Jefferson City
Mr. Randy H. Kollars
P.O. 417
Jefferson City, MO 65102

Diocese of Joliet
Sr. Sue Torgerson
430 N. Center
Joliet, IL 60435

Diocese of Juneau
Ms. Heidi H. Kirkevold
419 6th St. # 200
Juneau, AK 99801

Diocese of Kalamazoo
Mr. Ernest Bayer
215 N. Westnedge Ave.
Kalamazoo, MI 49005

Diocese of Kansas City -
 St. Joseph
Mr. Bill Cordaro
P.O. Box 419037
Kansas City, MO 64106

Archdiocese of Kansas City
 in Kansas
Mr. Dave Armstrong
12615 Parallel
Kansas City, KS 66109

Diocese of Knoxville
Rev. Jay Flaherty
201 Airport Rd.
Gatlinburg, TN 37738

Archdiocese of Los Angeles
Mr. Tom East
1531 W. Ninth St.
Los Angeles, CA 90015

Diocese of La Crosse
Mr. Dennis Kurtz
P.O. Box 1062
Eau Claire, WI 54702-1062

Diocese of Lafayette
Mr. Eugene Piccolo
2300 South Ninth St.
Lafayette, IN 47905

Diocese of Lafayette
Ms. Kathy Stelly
1408 Carmel Dr.
Lafayette, LA 70501

Diocese of Lake Charles
Mrs. Sandy Gay
P.O. Box 3223
Lake Charles, LA 70602

Diocese of Lansing
Mr. Brian Singer-Towns
228 North Walnut St.
Lansing, MI 48933

Diocese of Las Cruces
Ms. Annie M. Conway
1280 Med Park Dr.
Las Cruces, NM 88005-3239

Diocese of Lexington
Ms. Barbara Muray
1310 Leestown Rd.
Lexington, KY 40508

Diocese of Lincoln
Rev. Robert Barnhill
335 N. 27th St.
Lincoln, NE 68503

Diocese of Little Rock
Ms. Phyllis Enderlin
P.O. Box 7565
Little Rock, AR 72217

Archdiocese of Louisville
Mr. David Provost
1200 S. Shelby St.
Louisville, KY 40203

Diocese of Lubbock
Mr. Paul Florez
P.O. Box 98700
Lubbock, TX 79499-8700

Diocese of Madison
Katherine Kerkhof
142 W. Johnson St.
Madison, WI 53703-2295

Diocese of Manchester
Sr. Bernadette Turgeon
P.O. Box 310
153 Ash St.
Manchester NH 03104

Diocese of Marquette
Mr. Daniel Sparapani
347 Rock St.
Marquette, MI 49855

Diocese of Memphis
Rev. J. David Graham
203 S. White Station
Memphis, TN 38117

Archdiocese of Miami
Rev. Jose Espino
9401 Biscayne Blvd.
Miami, FL 33138

Archdiocese for Military Services
Ch. Col. (Msgr.) Owen Hendry
HQ AFMC/HC
Wright Patterson AFB
 OH 45433-5001

Diocese of Metuchen
Rev. Robert Lynam
436 Port Reading Ave.
Port Reading, NJ 07064

Archdiocese of Milwaukee
Mr. Thomas Tomaszek
3501 So. Lake Dr.
Milwaukee, WI 53207

Archdiocese of Mobile
Ms. McCorquordale
1413 Old Shell Rd.
Mobile, AL 36604

Diocese of Monterey
Sr. Dolores Fenzel
P.O. Box 350
Monterey, CA 93942

Diocese of Nashville
Rev. Joseph V. McMahon
6401 Harding Rd.
Nashville, TN 37205

Archdiocese of Newark
Rev. William J. Dowd
499 Belgrove Dr.
Kearny, NJ 07032

Archdiocese of New Orleans
Rev. Ronald Calkins
3801 Monroe St.
New Orleans, LA 70118

Archdiocese of New York
Rev. James Bolger - CYD
1011 First Ave.
New York, NY 10022

Diocese of New Ulm
Bill Casey
Catholic Pastoral Center
New Ulm, MN 56073

Diocese of Norwich
Mrs. Theo Hamell
1595 Norwich New Ldon Tpk.
Uncasville, CT 06382

Diocese of Oakland
Mr. Terry Koehne
521 Boden Way
Oakland, CA 94610

Archdiocese of Oklahoma City
Ms. Nancy Housh
P.O. Box 32180
Oklahoma City, OK 73123

Diocese of Ogdenburg
Rev. John R. Yonkouig
624 Washington St.
Ogdensburg, NY 13669

Archdiocese of Omaha
Rev. James Brown, O.A.R.
3300 North 60 St.
Omaha, NE 68104

Diocese of Orange
Mr. James Teixeira
2811 E. VillaReal
Orange, CA 92667

Diocese of Orlando
Ms. Marsha Hnat
P.O. Box 1800
Orlando, FL 32802

Diocese of Owensboro
Mr. Tony Cooper
600 Locust St.
Owensboro, KY 42301

Diocese of Palm Beach
Mrs. Karen Lower
9995 N. Military Trail
Palm Beach Gardens, FL 33410

Byzantine Eparchy of Parma
Ms. Theresa A. V. McDaniel
4600 State Rd.
Cleveland, OH 44109

Byzantine Diocese of Passaic
Rev. Robert Evancho
P.O. Box 206
Beaver Meadows, PA 18216

Diocese of Patterson
Rev. George F. Hundt
777 Valley Rd.
Clifton, NJ 07013

Diocese of Pensacola
Rev. Michael Cherup
P.O. Drawer 17329
Pensacola, FL 32522

Diocese of Peoria
Mr. Joe Ramirez
412 N.E. Madison
Peoria, IL 61550

Archdiocese of Philadelphia
Rev. Charles J. Pfeffer
105 Argyle Rd.
Ardmore, PA 19003

Diocese of Phoenix
Mr. Dennis Bozanich
400 East Monroe
Phoenix, AZ 85004

Diocese of Pittsburg
Ms. Joyce Gillooly
Gilmary Center
Flaugherty Run Rd.
Coraopolis, PA 15108

Byzantine Archdiocese of
    Pittsburgh
Rev. John Kudrick
225 Olivia St.
McKees Rocks, PA 15136

Archdiocese of Portland
Mr. Thomas Stein
2838 E. Burnside
Portland, OR 97214

Diocese of Portland
Mrs. Jeanne Bigelow
510 Ocean Ave.
Portland, Maine 04101

Diocese of Providence
Ms. Louise Dussault
One Cathedral Sq.
Providence, RI 02903-3695

Diocese of Pueblo
Mr. James Sciegel
1001 N. Grand Ave.
Pueblo, CO 81003

Diocese of Raleigh
Mr. Terence Jackson
300 Cardinal Gibbons Dr.
Raleigh, NC 27606

Diocese of Rapid City
Mr. David Lesmeister
P.O. Box 678
Rapid City, SD 57709

Diocese of Reno-Las Vegas
Rev. Patrick Leary
P.O. Box 18316
Las Vegas, NE 89114

Diocese of Richmond
Ms. Patricia Novak
811 Cathedral Pl.
Richmond, VA 23220

Diocese of Rockford
Ms. Barbara F. Campbell
1260 North Church St.
Rockford, Il 61103

Diocese of Rochester
Mr. Michael Thiesen
1150 Buffalo Rd.
Rochester, NY 14624

Diocese of Rockville
Mr. Michael McCarthy
99 North Village Ave.
Rockville Centre, NY 11570

Diocese of Sacramento
Ms. Cheryl Tholcke
2519 L St.
Sacramento, CA 95816

Diocese of Saginaw
Ms. Peggy McCourtney
5800 Weiss St.
Saginaw, MI 48603-2799

Diocese of Saint Cloud
Mr. Jeff Kaster
305 North 7th Ave.
St. Cloud, MN 56303

Diocese of Salina
Sr. Barbara Ellen
P.O. Box 980
Salina, KS 67402

Diocese of Salt Lake City
Mr. Paul Breaux
27 C St.
Salt Lake City, UT 84103

Diocese of San Angelo
Ms. Mary Sue Brewer
P.O. Box 1829
San Angelo, TX 76902

Diocese of San Bernardino
Ms. Grace Cassetta
6948 Elmwood Rd.
San Bernardino, CA 92404

Archdiocese of San Francisco
Ms. Louise J. Santiago
One St. Vincent Dr.
San Rafael, CA 94903

Diocese of San Antonio
Mr. Pat Perillo
P.O. Box 28410
San Antonio, TX 78228

Diocese of San Diego
Ms. Susan B. Stark
P.O. Box 85728
San Diego, CA 92186-5728

Diocese of San Jose
Mr. Robert Brancatelli
841 Lenzen Ave.
San Jose, CA 95126

Archdiocese of Santa Fe
Mrs. Bernadine Jaramillo
4000 St. Joseph's Pl., NW
Albuquerque, NM 87120

Diocese of Santa Rosa
Mr. Stanley Cordero
P.O. Box 11574
Santa Rosa, CA 95406

Diocese of Savannah
Mr. Julian Heyman
601 East Liberty St.
Savannah, GA 31401-5196

Diocese of Scranton
Ms. Kathy Yaklic
300 Wyoming Ave.
Scranton, PA 18503

Archdiocese of Seattle
Mr. Dave Jones
910 Marion St.
Seattle, WA 98104

Diocese of Shreveport
Mr. Donald Emge
2500 Line Ave.
Shreveport, LA 71104

Diocese of Sioux City
Fr. Edward Girres
P.O. Box 3379
Sioux City, IA 51102

Diocese of Sioux Falls
Ms. Nancy Werner
3100 W. 41st. St.
Sioux Falls, SD 57105

Diocese of Spokane
Ms. Linda Cooper
P.O. Box 1453
Spokane, WA 99210

Diocese of Springfield
Ms. Sylvia Murphy
625 Carew St.
Springfield, MA 01104

Diocese of Springfield in Illinois
Sr. Marilyn Jean Runkel, O.P.
1615 W. Washington Street
Springfield, IL 62708

Diocese of Springfield-Cape
   Girardeau
Sr. Rosalie Digenan
601 South Jefferson
Springfield, MO 65806

Diocese of Stamford
Rev. Jonathan Morse
161 Greenbrook Rd.
Stamford, CT 06902

Diocese of St. Augustine
Father John Tetlow
224 N. 5th St.
Jacksonville Beach, FL 32250

Byzantine Diocese of St. George
Rev. George Kuzara
721 Rural St.
Aurora, IL 60505

Diocese of St. Josaphat
Rev. Richard Seminack
730 Washington Ave.
Carnegie, PA 15106

Archdiocese of St. Louis
Mr. Thomas Merkel
4140 Lindell Blvd.
St. Louis, MO 63108

Diocese of St. Maron
Rev. David George
P.O. Box 2567
Brocton, MA 02405

Diocese of St. Nicholas
Ms. Sonia Peczeniuk
2245 W. Rice St.
Chicago, Il 60622

Archdiocese of St. Paul
Mr. Greg Weinand
2120 Park Ave.
Minneapolis, MN 55404

Diocese of St. Petersburg
Mr. Tom Miklusicak
P.O. Box 43022
St. Petersburg, FL 33743

Diocese of St. Thomas
Ms. Cynthia Smith
4081-Veterans Dr.
St. Thomas, USVI 00803

Diocese of Steubenville
Ms. Josetta Boeing, S.C.
422 Washington St.
Steubenville, OH 43952

Diocesan of Stockton
Mr. Michael Fields
1125 N. Lincoln St.
Stockton, CA 95203

Diocese of Superior
Mr. Roger Cadotte
Bishop Hammes Center
Haugen, WI 54841

Diocese of Syracuse
Rev. Robert B. Stephenson
240 E. Onondaga St.
Syracuse, NY 13202

Diocese of Toledo
Rev. Anthony Borgia
1601 Jefferson Ave.
Toledo, OH 43624

Diocese of Trenton
Rev. La Verghetta
50 Hurleys Lane
Lincroft, NJ 07738

Diocese of Tucson
Mr. Michael Berger
8800 E. 22nd St.
Tucson, AZ 85710

Diocese of Tulsa
Ms. Susan Koss
P.O. Box 2009
Tulsa, OK 7410

Diocese of Tyler
Ms. Sara Dwyer
1920 Sybil Lane
Tyler, TX 75703

Eparchy of Van Nuys
Rev. Joseph Hutsko
1074 S. Cook St.
Denver, CO 80209-4923

Diocese of Venice
Mrs. Patricia Hines
1000 Pinebrook Rd.
Venice, FL 34292

Diocese of Victoria
Mrs. Carolyn R. Adrian
P.O. Box 4070
Victoria, TX 77903

Archdiocese of Washington
Rev. John Dakes
P.O. Box 29260
Washington, DC 20017

Diocese of Wheeling
Mr. Michael Hall
P.O. Box 230
Wheeling, WV 26003

Diocese of Wichita
Ms. Clare Vanderpool
424 N. Brodway
Wichita, KS 67202

Diocese of Wilmington
Rev. John Hopkins
803 N. Broom St.
Wilmington, DE 19806

Diocese of Winona
Mr. John Vitek
P.O. Box 588
Winona, MN 55987

Diocese of Worcester
Rev. William Konicki
120 Hill St.
Whitinsville, MA 01588-1011

Diocese of Yakima
Father Kevin Minder
5301- A- Tieton Dr.
Yakima, WA 98908

Diocese of Youngstown
Rev. Kenneth E. Miller
144 West Wood St.
Youngstown, OH 44503

Some organizations working with the National Program Planning Committee that can assist groups with information about World Youth Day '93 are:

Ms. Beverly Carroll
Secretariat for Black Catholics
3211 Fourth St., NE
Washington D.C. 20017

Sr. Jane Nesmith
National African-American
Catholic Youth Ministry Network
5116 Magazine St.
New Orleans, LA 70115

Ms. Annetta Wilson
Knights of St. Peter Claver
Ladies Auxiliary
28 East Jackson Suite 610
Chicago, IL 60608

Wilson Boni
National Tekakwitha Conference
P.O. Box 6768
Great Falls, MT 59406-6759

Mr. Ron Cruz
Secretariat for Hispanic Affairs
3211 Fourth St., NE
Washington, DC 20017

Mr. Ron Cuadra
Southeast Regional Office
for Hispanic Affairs
2900 S.W. 87th Ave.
Miami, FL 33165

Ms. Carmen Castro
Northeast Hispanic Catholic Ctr.
1011 First Ave.
New York, NY 10022

Ms. Teresa Garza
Mid West Hispanic Catholic
Commission
P.O. Box 703
Notre Dame, Indiana 46556

Ms. Isabel Lumbreas
Northwest Regional Office
of Hispanic Affairs
220 Commercial St. NE
Salem, OR 97301

Mary Jane Owen
National Catholic Office for
Persons with Disabilities
P.O. Box 29113
Washington, DC 20017
202-529-2933 (v/TDY)

Ms. Noemi Castillo
Office for the Pastoral Care
of Migrants and Refugees
3211 Fourth St., NE
Washington, DC 20017

Mr. Frank Jimenez
Coordinator for Asian/Pacific
Affairs
50 Crestmont Rd.
West Orange, NJ 07052

Rev. Vincent Minh
Vietnamese Catholic Federation
of the USA
5404 NE Alameda Dr.
Portland, OR 97213

THE INTERNATIONAL GATHERING OF YOUNG ADULTS & YOUTH

THE POPE & YOUNG PEOPLE. TOGETHER

DENVER, CO , USA AUGUST 11-15

"I came so that they might have life and have it more abundantly."
John 10:10

How to use the Logo

Only dioceses, parishes, schools, and Catholic organizations with listing in P.J. Kennedy & Sons, *The Official Catholic Directory*, have permission to use the World Youth Day logo and the trademark name in the promotion of World Youth '93 in their own locality. The logo may only be used on written materials—i.e., news articles, bulletins, newsletters, flyers—and broadcasts about World Youth Day. No other entity or vendor may use the World Youth Day logo or trademark name without the prior written permission of World Youth Day, Inc., 3211 4th Street, N.E., Washington, D.C. 20017.

All rights to license or use the logo for any commercial purpose are retained by World Youth Day, Inc. The logo may not be printed on softgoods, pins, hats, etc., for sale or trade without prior written permission of World Youth Day, Inc., 3211 4th Street, N.E., Washington, D.C. 20017.

The logo may be reproduced in 3-colors (as illustrated on the front cover of this manual), one of three defined PMS colors, black, or white in a reversed situation. Reproduction of the logo in the 3 colors must adhere to PMS colors 226, 3145, and 376. The logo may not be reproduced using two colors.

Merchandising

Merchandise licensed through World Youth Day, Inc., will be available for fund-raising efforts at significant savings. Information on the exclusive line of merchandise is forthcoming in the November 1992 mailing.

Spanish Language Materials

Para Empezar:
Una Breve Historia

Al finalizar el Año Santo de 1984 el Santo Padre invitó a los jóvenes miembros de movimientos y asociaciones del mundo a ir a Roma para la ceremonia de clausura. En esa ocasión el Papa Juan Pablo II entregó a los jóvenes la Cruz del Año Santo como un recordatorio de su redención.

El año siguiente, el Santo Padre invitó a los jóvenes para que fueran a Roma el Domingo de Ramos y conmemorar el Año Internacional de la Juventud de las Naciones Unidas. Ese año, muchos jóvenes de los Estados Unidos se unieron a otros jóvenes del mundo, para celebrar su fe y su juventud. Muy pocos se dieron cuenta que participaban en el inicio de una magnífica tradición.

Para el Santo Padre ese encuentro con los jóvenes y una carta especial dirigida a ellos fueron más allá de la celebración de las Naciones Unidas y se han convertido en una celebración anual. Desde el 1985, el Papa Juan Pablo II ha dirigido una carta a los jóvenes del mundo y cada dos años (1985, 1987, 1989, 1991) los ha invitado a reunirse con él para catequizarlos, compartir la camaradería, el culto y la renovación. Estas reuniones han tenido lugar en Roma, Buenos Aires, Santiago de Compostela y Czestochowa.

El Domingo de Ramos de 1992, el Santo Padre anunció que el próximo encuentro internacional para la Jornada Mundial de la Juventud tendrá lugar en los Estados Unidos del 11 al 15 de agosto en la ciudad de Denver. En esa ocasión la misma Cruz que se había entregado a los jóvenes en 1984 fue presentada a un grupo de jóvenes de los Estados Unidos. El peregrinaje de esa Cruz por todos los Estados Unidos, empezando en Denver en agosto de 1993, simboliza nuestro peregrinar de fe.

La Jornada Mundial de la Juventud en los Estados Unidos

La celebración nacional para la Jornada Mundial de la Juventud se ha ido desarrollando paulatinamente. La conmemoración anual que tiene lugar el Domingo de Ramos en muchos países, aquí en los Estados Unidos era principalmente una misa en la catedral con el obispo. En el 1988, el Comité Administrativo de la Conferencia Nacional de Obispos Católicos (NCCB) decidió cambiar la fecha

de la celebración nacional para permitir que más parroquias y escuelas participaran y para no sobrecargar la celebración del Domingo de Ramos, la preparación para el Triduo Sagrado y el Domingo de Pascua. Después de consultar con la oficina litúrgica del NCCB se escogió el 30o Domingo Ordinario para la celebración que generalmente es el último domingo de octubre. Se seleccionó esa fecha debido a que tiene lecturas apropiadas y para no interfir con otras celebraciones/conmemoraciones nacionales.

En los Estados Unidos la celebración de la Jornada Mundial de la Juventud se ha dirigido a los adolescentes, los que están en escuelas intermedias y secundarias. Pero en Europa y en muchas otras partes del mundo es primariamente un día de celebración/conmemoración de los estudiantes universitarios y de los jóvenes adultos. Empezando en 1993 esperamos extender la celebración de los Estados Unidos a los estudiantes universitarios y a los jóvenes adultos para que el día sea también de ellos.

Aunque generalmente la conmemoración de la Jornada Mundial de la Juventud tiene lugar el 30o Domingo Ordinario, algunas diócesis tienen celebraciones el Domingo de Ramos. Esas diócesis inician eventos especiales que tendrán lugar durante el año y que concluirán el último domingo de octubre. No importa la fecha en que se celebre, lo que importa es que las diócesis, las parroquias y las escuelas celebren la Jornada Mundial de la Juventud. Hoy más que nunca, los jóvenes necesitan el apoyo y la afirmación de los padres y de la comunidad local.

En enero de 1991, los obispos de los Estados Unidos enviaron un mensaje pidiendo a todos los católicos, a todos el mundo — familias, iglesias, escuelas, gobiernos — que dieran prioridad en su tiempo, recursos, y energía a los niños y a los jóvenes. La Jornada Mundial de la Juventud puede ser un día para poner en alto a nuestra juventud, afirmar sus talentos y dones, para darles la bienvenida y acoger su participación en nuestras vidas y en la vida de nuestra Iglesia y nuestra sociedad.

Ciudades Claves en la Peregrinación

Para ayudar a los jóvenes en su camino a Denver, se ha establecido una red de Ciudades Claves. Grupos de peregrinos podrán solicitar comida y alojamiento en esas ciudades en su camino hacia Denver. La persona "contacto" de cada diócesis para la Jornada Mundial de la Juventud tendrá información sobre las Ciudades Claves y hará reservaciones. Hasta la fecha del 5 de septiembre de 1992 las ciudades claves son Boise, Idaho; Indianapolis, Indiana; Omaha, Nebraska; Salt Lake City, Utah; Rapid City, Iowa; Witchita, Kansas; Salinas, California; Albuquerque, New Mexico; y San Antonio, Texas. Se incluirán otras ciudades si es necesario.

La Cruz del Año Santo

La Cruz que el Santo Padre presentó a los jóvenes al finalizar el Año Santo de 1984 se ha convertido en un hermoso símbolo de la unidad de los jóvenes católicos y de la abundancia de la vida de Cristo. Esa misma Cruz fue entregada a un grupo de jóvenes de los Estados Unidos el 12 de abril de 1992, Domingo de Ramos. En preparación para la Jornada Mundial de la Juventud, la Cruz visitará varias localidades en el país. Es posible que la Cruz del Año Santo visite su área. La Cruz ha sido parte de todas las celebraciones internacionales de la Jornada Mundial de la Juventud que se han celebrado hasta ahora en Roma (1985), Buenos Aires (1987), Santiago de Compostela (1989) y Czestochowa (1991). En 1993 la Cruz del Año Santo será llevada a Denver para la Jornada Internacional. Si desea información sobre el itinerario de la Cruz del Año Santo llame a la oficina nacional de la Jornada Mundial de la Juventud al (202) 541-3001.

. . . . .

ALGUNAS PERSPECTIVAS IMPORTANTES

Hay varios temas y perspectivas que son la clave para una buena celebración de la Jornada Mundial de la Juventud. Recuérdelas en su planificación.

Evangelización y Servicio: Los Obispos de los Estados Unidos han pedido que el año de preparación se caracterice por la evangelización y el servicio. Ayuden a los jóvenes a aprender a cómo llegar a sus compañeros para evangelizarlos. Animen a los jóvenes a ser activos en el servicio a la comunidad, especialmente en un servicio que refleje la vida abundante que nos ofrece Jesús. Se puede tratar de establecer contacto con los jóvenes que sufren, los pobres o los que tienen gran necesidad de ser amados.

Inclusión Multicultural: Programas internacionales y nacionales tales como la Jornada Mundial de la Juventud nos dan la oportunidad de incluir experiencias de otras culturas en nuestros programas. Mientras que siempre debemos tratar de ayudar a los fieles a restablecer sus lazos culturales propios, debemos usar este tiempo en nuestra comunidad para apreciar y conocer los dones de otros culturas. Si pensamos en el racismo que existe en tantas personas e instituciones no es superfluo dedicar tiempo considerable a las experiencias interculturales.

Peregrinaciones: Peregrinar y orar se complementan mutuamente. Use esta oportunidad para ayudar a los jóvenes a entender la tradición de las peregrinaciones. Una peregrinación es un momento espiritual en nuestro caminar de fe que celebra un encuentro con Dios en el vivir diario y que culmina con la llegada a un lugar sagrado. Para más información sobre la peregrinación vea la página 81.

La Familia: El año en preparación para la Jornada Mundial de la Juventud tiene lugar en el año de la publicación de la declaración de los obispos *Los Niños y las Familias Primero: El reto para nuestra Iglesia, la Nación y el Mundo*; en el año del Congreso Nacional de la Familia Negra de 1992, (el tema fue La Familia Afro-Americana); y el año de la proclamación de las Naciones Unidas que 1994 será el Año de la Familia. La Jornada Mundial de la Juventud debe estar consciente de la familia y ofrecer respuestas a las necesidades de las familias.

La Iglesia, Comunidad Acogedora para Jóvenes y Jóvenes Adultos: Si los jóvenes y los jóvenes adultos no se sienten acogidos en nuestras parroquias, universidades y comunidades escolares durante este año de preparación para la Jornada Mundial de la Juventud, ¿se sentirán bienvenidos alguna vez? Permita que los jóvenes y los jóvenes adultos sean vistos en la comunidad. Ofrézcales oportunidades para contribuir a dar forma a la parroquia o a la vida universitaria. Sobre todo, incluya a los jóvenes y a los jóvenes adultos en la planificación de la Jornada Mundial de la Juventud. El año de preparación presenta una oportunidad magnífica para que la parroquia y la universidad inicien el ministerio con y para los jóvenes y los jóvenes adultos, si no existe.

La Jornada Mundial de la Juventud presenta, de manera especial, un reto a los adultos en la Iglesia para descubrir los dones de la juventud. Nuestros jóvenes tienen mucho que dar a la Iglesia y a nuestra sociedad y debemos estar abiertos para descubrir los dones que hay entre ellos.

Sean Buenos Administradores de la Tierra: La Jornada Mundial de la Juventud de 1993 tendrá un gran impacto en toda la nación y especialmente en

Denver. Estén conscientes de preservar los recursos naturales, pensando en la tierra y tratando bien a todas las creaturas que habitan en ella.

PEREGRINACIÓN Y LA JORNADA MUNDIAL DE LA JUVENTUD

"Es una peregrinación en la década del 90 con "sneakers" remplazando las sandalias y el transporte moderno substituyendo a camellos y caballos. Supongo que muchos jóvenes vendrán a pie y en bicicleta. No importa cómo vengan, los jóvenes encontrarán a Dios cerca de las casi eternas montañas.

Arzobispo William Keeler Baltimore

(Paul Henderson)

Peregrino, Peregrinación... son palabras que tienen diferente significado para diferentes personas. En los Estados Unidos los que emigraron de Europa ven la palabra en relación a su historia. La Roca de Plymouth y el Día de Acción de Gracias simbolizan y celebran a los Peregrinos que cruzaron el Atlántico buscando una nueva vida y un nuevo mundo. Nuestros antepasados que formaron parte de la expansión hacia el oeste también usaron la palabra peregrinos para describir a los que se establecieron en las tierras lejanas. Los Americanos Nativos recuerdan a los peregrinos de manera diferente y ven al peregrino de Europa como invasor. Para algunas tribus, peregrinación evoca imágenes dolorosas de un asentamiento forzado. Los teólogos hablan de un iglesia peregrina y se refieren a los creyentes como un pueblo peregrino. Pasamos por este mundo como peregrinos en peregrinación hacia la promesa de la vida eterna. Los cristianos mantienen una tradición muy rica de peregrinación a muchos lugares sagrados y a santuarios, pero no somos los únicos. Los musulmanes y los judíos también valoran mucho la tradición de las peregrinaciones.

En preparación para la Jornada Mundial de la Juventud, debemos estar atentos a la dimensión de peregrinación. Aunque el destino de una peregrinación es casi siempre una iglesia, santuario u otro lugar sagrado donde la presencia de Dios se ha manifestado de manera especial, la peregrinación a Denver tendrá además otro punto central. Todos los que viajen a Denver serán invitados a una peregrinación a la Catedral de la Inmaculada Concepción. Pero los peregrinos de la Jornada Mundial de la Juventud también serán invitados a peregrinar al santuario de la persona. Podemos estar seguros de que Dios se manifiesta en el corazón de los jóvenes que se reunirán en fe al pié de las

montañas de Colorado.

En sus preparaciones para la Jornada Mundial de la Juventud recuerden:

1. Enseñar sobre las peregrinaciones. Aunque hay diferentes conceptos es importante que los participantes entiendan nuestra tradición católica.

2. Dar a los jóvenes la oportunidad de participar en una peregrinación local. Una peregrinación en el área local ayudará a los participantes a prepararse para su experiencia en Denver, y también será una oportunidad para que los jóvenes continúen su renovación espiritual después que regresen a sus hogares.

3. Hacer del viaje a Denver una peregrinación y no una convención. Somos un pueblo peregrino caminando para acercarnos a Dios. Aproveche las ermitas o santuarios que hay en las ciudades claves en la ruta de viaje. Incluya oración y planeen para las dificultades del viaje.

El significado de peregrinar

La palabra peregrinaje puede ser extraña a los oídos de muchos. En este país la gente tiene más familiaridad con actividades y movimientos tales como la Marcha por la Vida, caminatas, desfiles y viajes de turismo en las vacaciones. Una peregrinación es una experiencia totalmente diferente. Se podría decir que una peregrinación es un viaje que se hace a una iglesia, santuario o a otro lugar sagrado por motivos espirituales. Los elementos esenciales de una peregrinación son:

A. Motivación espiritual — Tener una motivación espiritual es parte esencial de una peregrinación. Una persona decide llevar a cabo una peregrinación para lograr un fin espiritual: dar gracias a Dios por las gracias recibidas, expiar por sus pecados, la conversión personal o por devoción. Por tanto una peregrinación es muy diferente a un viaje de turismo. Los turistas ven con los ojos mientras que los peregrinos ven con el corazón. Una peregrinación es, sobre todo, el deseo de acercarse más al Dios Trinitario — Padre, Hijo y Espíritu Santo — e implica poder soportar alguna dificultad, sufrimiento o pena para lograr el crecimiento interior.

B. *El viaje* — En cada peregrinación siempre hay movimiento de un lugar a otro, no sólo caminar. Salir de viaje, cambiar nuestras rutinas y nuestro ambiente para visitar un lugar diferente no sólo tienen beneficios psicológicos sino también significado espiritual. Con mucha frecuencia, Jesús llevaba a sus discípulos a sitios apartados para descansar, meditar y compartir con ellos los misterios del Reino.

Generalmente, una peregrinación es un grupo de personas que viajan hacia un determinado destino. Una peregrinación individual es también muy común. En el camino, se siguen ciertos ritos con oración, reflexión y cantos. Una peregrinación puede enriquecerse con un descubrimiento personal como les sucedió a los apóstoles en el camino de Emaús. Caminar juntos, compartir y orar crean sentido de comunidad. Una peregrinación no es algo totalmente separado de la vida de la Iglesia, ni es tampoco algo que se hace por si solo, o que termina cuando el viaje ha concluido. La vida toda es una peregrinación hacia Dios. Como dice el himno de los Encuentros: "Somos un pueblo que camina ...."

C. *Lugar Sagrado* — El destino de una peregrinación deberá siempre ser un santuario u otro lugar sagrado en el cual se cree que Dios se ha manifestado de manera especial. Las peregrinaciones regularmente se hacen a lugares relacionados con la vida de Cristo (por ej., la Tierra Santa), de la Santísima Virgen o de los Santos. Estos lugares se denominan santuarios o ermitas porque allí la gente encuentra la presencia de Dios de una manera muy personal.

Desde la reunión en Roma durante el Año Internacional de la Juventud declarado por las Naciones Unidas en 1985, el espíritu de peregrinación ha sido parte de estas reuniones internacionales. Las peregrinaciones son experiencias comunes y parte de la vida religiosa de la Iglesia en Europa, América Latina, y en el Canadá francés. El valor de una peregrinación, su relación a la vida cotidiana y su impacto en la vida individual de la comunidad puede cultivarse en los Estados Unidos. En el Sureste y en el Suroeste de los Estados Unidos, entre los cubanos y los méjico-americanos hay ermitas y santuarios que reciben miles de peregrinos anualmente.

Peregrinación de la Cruz

La Jornada Mundial de la Juventud de 1993 en Denver nos ofrece una buena oportunidad para presentar a los jóvenes la experiencia de una peregrinación como preparación para su encuentro con el Santo Padre y con otros peregrinos del mundo entero.

Para facilitar la experiencia, la Cruz del Año Santo viajará por todos las diócesis de los Estados Unidos. Se ha creado un rito especial para ayudar con la preparación para la visita de la Cruz en cada diócesis y para promover otras actividades relacionadas con la Jornada Mundial de la Juventud. Para más información sobre la visita de la Cruz a su comunidad puede llamar a la oficina de la Jornada Mundial de la Juventud 1 (202)541-3001.

Varios santuarios han ofrecido ayuda espiritual a los que hagan la peregrinación a Denver. La hospitalidad y calurosa bienvenida que se le ofrecerá a los jóvenes en esos santuarios ayudará a intensificar el significado de su peregrinación.

Para que el viaje a Denver sea una verdadera peregrinación se necesita hacer preparaciones especiales. Una peregrinación no empieza el día que se inicia el viaje sino que requiere estrategia y planificación, y la cooperación de todos los participantes.

Las actividades de la Jornada Mundial de la Juventud en Denver durante la reunión internacional incluirán una peregrinación en el programa de actividades. Se designarán varias rutas donde los jóvenes de todo el mundo tendrán la oportunidad de hacer una peregrinación a varios santuarios en su camino hacia Denver y a la Catedral de la Inmaculada Concepción en el la misma ciudad de Denver. También habrá una peregrinación el sábado, 14 de agosto de 1993, desde los diversos sitios asignados para la catequesis hasta el lugar donde el Santo Padre oficiará la vigilia del sábado y la misa del domingo.

Se recomienda que los jóvenes se preparan espiritual y físicamente para su peregrinación.

Podrá obtener más información sobre los preparativos para la Jornada Mundial de la Juventud mediante la oficina de la persona contacto en su diócesis. Llame a su oficina diocesana para informarse sobre el nombre de esa persona o a la oficina nacional en el 202-541-3001.

• • • • •

Mensaje a los Jóvenes y a las Jóvenes del Mundo Con Ocasión de la VIII Jornada Mundial de la Juventud -1993

Yo he venido para que tengan vida y la tengan en abundancia (Jn 10:10)

¡Muy queridos jóvenes!

1. Después de los encuentros de Roma, de Buenos Aires, de Santiago de Compostela y de Czestochowa, sigue nuestra peregrinación sobre los caminos de la historia contemporánea. La próxima etapa será en Denver, en el corazón de los Estados Unidos, junto a las Montañas Rocosas de Colorado, donde, en agosto de 1993, se celebrará la VIII Jornada Mundial de la Juventud. Allí, junto a tantos jóvenes americanos, se darán cita, como ya ha sucedido en los encuentros anteriores, chicos y chicas de todo el mundo, representando la fe más viva o, al menos, la búsqueda más apasionada del universo juvenil de los cinco continentes.

Estas manifestaciones periódicas no quieren ser un rito convencional, es decir, un acontecimiento que se justifica en su misma repetición. Al contrario, nacen más bien de una necesidad profunda que tiene su origen en el corazón del ser humano y se refleja en la vida del la Iglesia, peregrina y misionera.

Las Jornadas y los Encuentros Mundiales de la Juventud marcan providenciales momentos de reflexión: ayudan a los jóvenes a interrogarse sobre sus aspiraciones más íntimas, a profundizar su sentido eclesial, a proclamar con crecientes gozo y audacia la común fe en Cristo, muerto y resucitado. Son momentos en los que muchos de ellos maduran opciones valientes e iluminadas, que pueden contribuir a orientar el futuro de la historia bajo la guía, al mismo tiempo fuerte y suave, del Espíritu Santo.

En el mundo presenciamos la sucesión de los imperios, es decir, la sucesión de intentos de unidad política que determinados hombres imponen a otros hombres. Los resultados están a la vista de todos. No es posible construir una verdadera y constante unidad mediante la constricción y la violencia. Una meta tan alta sólo se puede alcanzar construyendo sobre el fundamento de un común patrimonio de valores acogidos y compartidos, como, por ejemplo, el respeto a la dignidad del ser humano, la acogida de la vida, la defensa de los derechos humanos, la apertura a la transcendencia y a las dimensiones del espíritu.

En esta perspectiva, respondiendo a los desafíos del tiempo que cambia, el encuentro mundial de los jóvenes quiere ser semilla y propuesta de una nueva unidad, que transciende el orden político, pero que lo ilumina. Se funda en la certeza de que sólo el Artífice del corazón humano puede dar una respuesta adecuada a los deseos que en él se albergan. De esta forma la Jornada Mundial de la Juventud se convierte también en el anuncio de Cristo que proclama a los hombres de este siglo: Yo he venido para que tengan vida y la tengan en abundancia (Jn 10:10).

2. Entramos así de lleno en el tema que guiará la reflexión durante este año de preparación a la próxima Jornada.

En todas las lenguas existen varios términos para expresar lo que el hombre no quiere perder bajo ningún concepto, lo que constituye su aspiración, su deseo, su esperanza; pero ninguna otra palabra como el término vida logra resumir en todas ellas de forma tan completa las mayores aspiraciones del ser humano. Vida indica la suma de los bienes deseados y al mismo tiempo aquello que los hace posibles, accesibles, duraderos.

¿Acaso la historia del hombre no está marcada por una fatigosa y dramática búsqueda de algo o alguien que sea capaz de liberarlo de la muerte y de asegurarle la vida?

La existencia humana conoce momentos de crisis y de cansancio, de desilusión y de oscuridad. Se trata de una experiencia de insatisfacción que se refleja bien en tanta literatura y en tanto cine de nuestros días. A la luz de un esfuerzo tan grande es fácil comprender la particular dificultad de los adolescentes y de los jóvenes que se dirigen, con el corazón encogido, hacia ese conjunto de promesas fascinantes y de oscuras incógnitas que presenta la vida.

Jesús ha venido para dar la repuesta definitiva al deseo de vida y de lo infinito que el Padre celeste, creándonos, ha inscrito en nuestro ser. En la culminación de la revelación, el Verbo encarnado proclama: "Yo soy la vida" (Jn 14:6), y también: "Yo he venido para que tengan vida" (Jn 10:10). ¿Pero qué vida? La intención de Jesús es clara — la misma vida de Dios, que está por encima de todas las aspiracines que pueden nacer en el corazón humano (cfr. 1 Cor 2:9). Efectivamente, por la gracia del Bautismo, nosotros ya somos hijos de Dios (cfr. 1 Jn 3:1-2).

Jesús ha salido al encuentro de los hombres, ha curado a enfermos y a los que sufren, ha liberado a endemoniados y resucitado a muertos. Se ha entregado a sí mismo en la cruz y ha resucitado, manifestándose de esta forma como el Señor de la vida, autor y fuente de la vida inmortal.

3. La experiencia cotidiana nos enseña que la vida está marcada por el pecado y amenazada por la muerte, a pesar de la sed de bondad que late en nuestro corazón y del deseo de vida que recorre nuestros miembros. Por poco que estemos atentos a nosotros mismos y a las situaciones que la existencia nos presenta, descubrimos que todo dentro de nosotros nos empuja más allá de nosotros mismos, todo nos invita a superar la tentación de la superficialidad o de la desesperación. Es entonces cuando el ser humano está llamado a hacerse discípulo de aquel Otro que lo transciende infinitamente, para entrar finalmente en la vida eterna.

Existen falsos profetas y falsos maestros de vida. Hay maestros que enseñan a salir del cuerpo, del tiempo y del espacio para poder entrar en la vida verdadera. Estos condenan la creación y, en nombre de un falso espiritualismo, conducen a miles de jóvenes por caminos de una liberación imposible, que al final los deja más solos, víctimas del propio engaño y del propio mal.

Aparentemente en el polo opuesto, los maestros del carpe diem (gozo inmediato) invitan a seguir toda inclinación o apetencia instintiva, con el resultado de hacer caer al individuo en una angustia llena de inquietud, acompañada de peligrosas evasiones hacia falaces paraísos artificiales como el de la droga.

También hay maestros que sitúan el sentido de la vida exclusivamente en el éxito, en el deseo de riquezas, en el desarrollo de las capacidades personales, sin tener en cuenta la existencia de los otros ni el respeto por los valores, ni siquiera por el valor fundamental de la vida.

Estos y otros tipos de falsos maestros de vida, numerosos también en el mundo contemporáneo, proponen objetivos que no sólo no sacian, sino que agudizan y aumentan la sed que arde en el alma del hombre. ¿Quién podrá por tanto medir y colmar sus deseos? ¿Quién, sino Aquel que, siendo el autor de la vida, puede saciar el deseo que El mismo ha puesto dentro de su corazón? El se acerca a cada uno para proponerle el anuncio de una esparanza que no engaña; El, que es al mismo tiempo el camino y la vida: el camino para entrar en la vida.

Nosotros solos no sabremos realizar aquello para lo que hemos sido creados. En nosotros hay una promesa, pero nos descubrimos impotentes para realizarla. Sin embargo el Hijo de Dios, que vino entre los hombres, dijo: Yo soy el camino, la verdad y la vida (Jn 14:6). Según una sugestiva expresión de San Agustín, Cristo ha querido crear un lugar donde cada hombre pueda encontrar la vida verdadera. Este lugar es su Cuerpo y su Espíritu, en el que toda la realidad humana, redimida y perdonada, se renueva y diviniza.

4. Efectivamente, la vida de cada uno de nosotros ha sido pensada antes de la creación del mundo, y con razón podemos reperir con el salmista: Señor, tú me sondeas y me conoces. . .tú has creado mis entrañas, me has tejido en el seno materno (Sal 139).

Esta vida, que estaba en Dios desde el principio (cfr. Jn 1:4), es vida que se entrega, que nada retiene para sí y que, sin cansarse, libremente se comunica. Es luz, la luz verdadera que ilumina a todo hombre (Jn 1:9). Es Dios, que vino a poner su tienda entre nosotros (cfr. Jn 1:14) para indicarnos el camino de la inmortalidad propia de los hijos de Dios y para hacerlo accesible.

En el misterio de su cruz y de su resurrección, Cristo ha destruido la muerte y el pecado, ha abolido la distancia infinita que existía entre cada hombre y la vida nueva en él. "Yo soy la resurrección y la vida" - Él proclama - "quien cree en mí, aunque muera, vivirá; y todo el que vive y cree en mí, no morirá jamás" (Jn 11:25).

Cristo realiza todo esto donando su Espíritu, dador de vida, en los sacramentos; particularmente en el Bautismo, sacramento que hace de la existencia recibida de los padres, frágil y destinada a la muerte, un camino hacia la eternidad; en el sacramento de la Penitencia que renueva continuamente la vida divina gracias al perdón de los pecados; en la Eucaristía pan de vida (cfr. Jn 6:34), que alimenta a los vivos y hace firmes sus pasos en la peregrinación terrena, hasta poder llegar a decir con el apóstol San Pablo: "Y vivo, pero no yo, sino que es Cristo quien vive en mí." (Gal 2:20).

5. La vida nueva, don del Señor resucitado, se irradia después a todos los ámbitos de la experiencia humana: en la familia, en la escuela, en el trabajo, en las activdades de todos los días y en el tiempo libre.

La vida nueva comienza a florecer aquí y ahora. Signo de su presencia y de su crecimiento es la caridad: Nosotros sabemos que hemos pasado de la muerte a la vida — afirma San Juan — porque amamos a nuestros hermanos (1 Jn 3:14) con un amor de obra y en verdad. La vida florece en el don de sí a los otros, según la vocación de cada uno: en el sacerdocio ministerial, en la virginidad consagrada, en el matrimonio, de modo que todos puedan, con actitud solidaria, compartir los dones recibidos, sobre todo con los pobres y los necesitados.

Aquel que nazca de lo alto será capaz se ver el Reino de Dios (cfr. Jn 3:3) y de comprometerse en la construcción de estructuras sociales más dignas de los seres humanos y de cada individuo, en la promoción y defensa de la cultura de la vida contra cualquier amenaza de muerte.

6. Queridos jóvenes, vosotros os hacéis intérpretes de una pregunta que, frecuentemente, os hacen

muchos de vuestros amigos: ¿Cómo y dónde podemos encontrar esta vida? ¿Cómo y dónde podremos vivirla?

La respuesta la podéis encontrar vosotros mismos, si tratáis de permanecer fielmente en el amor de Cristo (cfr. Jn 15:9). Vosotros podréis experimentar directamente la verdad de su palabra: "Yo soy... la vida" (Jn. 14:6). y podréis llevar a todos este gozoso anuncio de esperanza. El os ha constituido sus embajadores, primeros evangelizadores de vuestros semejantes.

La próxima Jornada Mundial de la Juventud en Denver nos ofrecerá una ocasión propicia para reflexionar juntos sobre este tema de gran interés para todos. Pero hay que prepararse para esta importante cita, mirar a nuestro alrededor para encontrar y reconocer aquellos lugares en los que Cristo está presente como manantial de vida. Pueden ser las comunidades parroquiales, los grupos y movimientos de apostolado, los monasterios y casas religiosas, y tambíen personas concretas a través de las cuales, como sucedió a los discípulos de Emaús, El hace que arda nuestro corazón y se abra a la esperanza.

Queridos jóvenes, con espíritu de generosidad, sentíos directamente implicados en la tarea de la nueva evangelización, que compromete a todos. Anunciad a Cristo que murió por todos a fin de que los que viven no vivan ya para ellos sino para el que murió y resucitó por ellos. (2 Cor 5:15).

7. A vosotros, muy queridos jóvenes de los Estados Unidos, que daréis hospitalidad a la próxima Jornada Mundial de la Juventud, se os ha concedido la alegría de acoger como un don del Espíritu el encuentro con tantos jóvenes que desde todos los lugares del mundo llegarán como peregrinos a vuestro país.

Ya os estáis preparando para ello mediante una gran actividad espiritual y organizativa, en la que están implicados todos los miembros de vuestras comunidades eclesiales.

Deseo de corazón que un acontecimiento tan extraordinario contribuya a acrecentar en cada uno el entusiasmo y la fidelidad en el seguimiento de Cristo y a acoger con gozo su mensaje, fuente de vida nueva.

Os confío a la protección de la Santísima Virgen, por medio de la cual hemos recibido al autor de la vida, Jesucristo, Hijo de Dios y Señor nuestro. Con gran afecto os bendigo a todos.

Vaticano, 15 de agosto de 1992, solemnidad de la Asunción de María Santísima.
Juan Pablo II

. . . . .

Definición Del Ministerio Para Jóvenes

Adoptado por la Junta Nacional de la Asociación para el Ministerio a los Jóvenes

¿Quiénes Son los Jóvenes?

La juventud abarca una población grande, diversa y en movimiento constante, que generalmente alcanza desde los adolescentes mayores hasta los adultos de 35 años. El término "joven adulto" no se refiere solamente a cierta edad, sino que describe un paso, una actitud, una orientación, una experiencia de vida. La juventud es esa etapa de la vida en la que se busca dirección, en la que las opciones son probadas y durante la cual se hacen compromisos. (United States Catholic Conference, *Planning for Single Young Adult Ministry: Directions for Minsterial Outreach.* Washington, D.C.: USCC, 1981, 10).

Se pueden encontrar adultos en todos los estados de vida y en cada comunidad de nuestra sociedad desde los campos y los pueblos pequeños, hasta las grandes ciudades. Representan diversas estructuras educacionales, vocacionales, sociales, políticas, culturales y espirituales. Ya sean solteros o casados, con o sin hijos, la juventud no puede estereotiparse.

Dentro de la "primera adultez" se pueden identificar tres etapas de desarrollo que requieren diferentes tareas. El paso por esas etapas depende de la condición de vida y de la cultura específica de los jóvenes.

La primera etapa ocurre en los años inmediatamente antes y después de los veinte cuando el desarrollo de la identidad personal, el establecimiento de una relación íntima con Dios y con otras personas y la exploración de posibles carreras profesionales son las tareas vitales. Los compromisos a corto plazo son más aptos para los jóvenes en esa etapa debido a la variedad de opciones que tienen por delante.

Hay muchos jóvenes que tienen gran fe pero frecuentemente no practican su fe en la manera tradicional hasta que pasan a la próxima etapa que regularmente ocurre alrededor de los 25 años. En esa etapa las tareas vitales incluyen opciones profesionales y su establecimiento dentro de una carrera específica y la selección de un modo de vida más permanente. Los jóvenes adultos empiezan a ligarse a la vida de una parroquia en busca de una experiencia significativa del culto o una comunidad de fe acogedora. Están comprometidos a buscar el significado de la vida, la verdad y la autenticidad.

Cuando los jóvenes adultos alcanzan el final de la década de los veinte y el principio de los treinta

empiezan a buscar una comunidad donde puedan echar raíces pero que los afirme y los rete al mismo tiempo. Son capaces de hacer compromisos más permanentes, usan sus experiencias previas para hacer decisiones sobre el futuro, hacen una contribución al mundo y se vuelven más activos en la vida parroquial. (USCC, *Young Adult Ministry Resources.* Washington, D.C.: USCC, 1988, 35-37).

No se puede olvidar que para muchos jóvenes adultos la principal tarea en la vida es poder sobrevivir.

¿Qué es el Ministerio con Jóvenes Adultos?

Para definir este ministerio hay que ver la experiencia de nuestro Maestro Jesucristo que ejerció el ministerio mediante la palabra y el ejemplo. Su predicación buscaba la acción con sus enseñanzas sobre el Reino de Dios que ya había llegado. Sus acciones siempre ofrecían una respuesta. Jesús descubrió las necesidades de los que acudieron a él y las atendió. Al dar respuesta a los que acudían a él, nos enseñó a responder a las necesidades de los demás.

El ministerio juvenil es una respuesta a las necesidades de los jóvenes adultos, una invitación a compartir sus talentos con el resto de la comunidad, un reto a vivir los valores del Evangelio en el mundo. Dentro de la diócesis, la parroquia o uno a uno, los ministros de los jóvenes caminan junto a los jóvenes para que puedan más fácilmente responsabilizarse por su vida de fe, construir comunidad en una Iglesia con personas de varias generaciones y crecer espiritualmente. Los ministros colaboran con los jóvenes adultos para despertar en ellos su llamado bautismal a ser discípulos, y para darles dirección. Mediante ministerios sociales, educacionales y varios servicios se inicia un proceso para ayudar a los jóvenes a tomar responsabilidad en el ministerio. En vez de ofrecer una serie de programas predeterminados, el proceso evoluciona y cambia con los jóvenes que desarrollan el ministerio. Los talentos y dones que ellos descubren afirman a los jóvenes y les animan a continuar la misión de construir el reino.

Principios Fundamentales

1. El ministerio a las jóvenes se basa en Jesucristo, que con su vida, muerte y resurrección es la revelación de Dios entre nosotros que mediante el Espíritu Santo se hace presente constantemente.

2. El ministerio a los jóvenes se vive en el discipulado cristiano mediante el cual crece y se sostiene la relación personal con Dios en Jesucristo.

3. El ministerio a los jóvenes nace de la vida y misión de la Iglesia que son los medios para continuar la presencia y la obra de Jesús en el mundo.

4. El ministerio a los jóvenes está dentro del contexto de la formación vital que nutre la vida cristiana mediante la confianza, la fe y la acción.

5. El ministerio a los jóvenes los llama a adquirir sentido de la vocación en la tarea de llevar su presencia y dedicación cristiana al mundo y al ambiente en que se desenvuelven sus talentos.

6. El ministerio a los jóvenes reconoce a los jóvenes adultos como parte del sistema de familia y a la familia como la primera Iglesia. Cualquier experiencia dentro del sistema facilitará o impedirá el crecimiento de la persona.

7. El ministerio a los jóvenes reconoce y acepta las diferencias entre jóvenes adultos en áreas rurales, urbanas y suburbanas y entre varios grupos étnicos y raciales, niveles económicos y situaciones de vida. Quiere responder a las necesidades de cada uno y darle oportunidad para que puedan alcanzar la plenitud de la madurez cristiana.

8. El ministerio a los jóvenes valora las expresiones culturales específicas de la fe de los jóvenes adultos y cree que la fe enriquece a la cultura y la cultura influye en la fe.

Principios Operacionales

1. Debido a que hay tantos jóvenes adultos en nuestras comunidades, las iglesias que desean

atraerlos les dan la bienvenida, ofrecen buenas liturgias y les invitan a participar en tareas importantes y visibles (en la liturgia, juntas, etc.).

2. Debido a que hay tantos jóvenes adultos que no asisten a la liturgia dominical, este ministerio debe estar caracterizado por la hospitalidad y el deseo de llegar a ellos.

3. Debido a que los jóvenes adultos son tan diversos (en edad, cultura y antecedentes familiares), los ministerios para ellos tienen que dar respuestas apropiadas mediante servicios, estilos y horarios variados.

4. Debido a que la etapa de la juventud es un tiempo para probar y hacer compromisos, los ministerios para ellos deben ofrecer varias opciones y flexibilidad.

5. Debido a que la etapa de la juventud es un tiempo de dar sentido a la vida, la Iglesia reconoce la necesidad de reunir a los jóvenes para compartir el pan y contar sus historias dentro de una comunidad de confianza. Allí es dónde los buenos escuchas descubren las necesidades, visiones e ideales de la juventud.

6. Debido a que el ministerio a los jóvenes adultos se debe desenvolver dentro de un esquema completo incluirá oración, acompañamiento, escuchar, sanar, facilitar e integrar. (USCC, Planning for Single Young Adult Ministry: Directions for Ministerial Outreach. Washington, D.C. USCC, 18-21).

7. Debido a que los jóvenes adultos frecuentemente están busca de la fe, el ministerio a los jóvenes utiliza modelos de formación adulta y ofrece un lugar dónde se sienten cómodos para cuestionar, dudar, luchar, entender y aceptar.

8. Debido a que sus vidas están centradas en las relaciones, los jóvenes adultos deben ser servidos dentro de un contexto de relaciones y se le deben ofrecer modelos y mentores. Cada comunidad es responsable de identificar una persona de fácil acceso y calificada (asalariada o voluntaria) como contacto para servir a las necesidades de los jóvenes y para proporcionar continuidad.

9. Debido a que los jóvenes adultos son receptivos a los medios de comunicación, hay que ser creativos y usar imágenes vivas como complemento efectivo a nuestra invitación personal.

10. Debido a que los jóvenes adultos pasan gran parte de su tiempo en medio de una sociedad altamente competitiva y consumista, la Iglesia necesita presentar su evaluación de esa sociedad y ofrecer otro sistema de valores para ayudarlos a hacer decisiones éticas y a elegir su vocación.

11. Debido a que los jóvenes adultos frecuentemente vuelven a la Iglesia en momentos de cambio o de crisis (a veces dentro del contexto de uno de los sacramentos), los líderes eclesiales necesitan ser sensitivos, estar abiertos a sus necesidades y ser acogedores.

12. Debido a que los jóvenes adultos entran en contacto con la Iglesia en situaciones variadas y debido a que el ministerio es un trabajo en colaboración, el ministerio de jóvenes adultos trata de organizarse simultáneamente en varias áreas (la parroquia, grupos de parroquias, la ciudad, la diócesis, etc.) y comparte los recursos con un variedad de organizaciones (RCIA, educación de adultos, ministerio universitario, etc).

13. Debido a que muchos jóvenes adultos muestran interés en mejorar la situación de los pobres y de los oprimidos, y debido a que esta tarea es central al Evangelio, nuestro ministerio los mueve a responder a las necesidades humanas y a confrontar aquellas instituciones y estructuras que promueven la injusticia.

14. Debido a que los jóvenes adultos viven en una sociedad con diversas religiones (muy aparente en el alto número de matrimonios entre personas de diferentes credos, el ministerio de jóvenes adultos debe estar consciente de esa realidad.

. . . . .

Sugerencias para la Planificación Litúrgica

1. Trabajen con el Comité Litúrgico de la parroquia para desarrollar un plan que ayude a reflejar el Año de Preparación para la Jornada Mundial de la Juventud durante el 1993 y que

incorpore el tema propuesta por el Santo Padre: "Yo he venido para que tengan vida y la tengan en abundancia" (Jn 10:10). Algunas ideas son:

Aunque el tema de cada misa es el Misterio Pascual, el comité litúrgico podría enfocar la vida abundante que se nos ofrece mediante la muerte y resurrección de Jesús.

Hacer mención frecuente de la Jornada Mundial de la Juventud en la Oración de los Fieles.

La asamblea podría contribuir a una colecta de artículos que la comunidad daría a una organización cuyo trabajo es una extensión de la vida abundante de Cristo. Por ejemplo: comida, ropa, artículos para la higiene personal, medicina, juguetes, libros, manualidades, cartas de apoyo, etc.

El comité de liturgia puede invitar a los jóvenes y a los jóvenes adultos a ser ministros de la liturgia en este Año de Preparación.

Se podría colocar un estandarte en la iglesia que refleje el tema de la Jornada Mundial basado en el Evangelio del Cuarto Domingo de Pascua (Juan 10:1-10). La parroquia podría usar ese domingo para resaltar la Jornada Mundial de la Juventud y orar por el triunfo de ese encuentro. Se podría ofrecer una bendición especial para todos aquellos que están preparándose espiritualmente para ir a Denver.

2. La parroquia podría designar un fin de semana específico como Domingo para Volver al Hogar Espiritual. Se trataría de ofrecer una invitación a los jóvenes y a los jóvenes adultos para regresar a la Iglesia. Esto se podría hacer antes de la reunión de Denver o en el otoño de 1993.

3. Se podría preparar una exhibición en el vestíbulo de la iglesia de jóvenes y jóvenes adultos en la parroquia. La exhibición podría mostrar como la juventud refleja la vida abundante que Jesús nos ofrece.

4. Jóvenes de la parroquia podrían escribir una seri de reflexiones para ser publicadas en el boletín parroquial.

5. Meditaciones personales podrían ser incluidas en el boletín durante los domingos de mayo en los que las lecturas del Evangelio hablan de la nueva vida representada en Jesús.

6. Se podría decir una oración especial en primer domingo del año para conmemorar el principio del año de preparación.

7. Jóvenes de la parroquia podrían distribuir la oración de la Jornada Mundial de la Juventud a la entrada de la iglesia.

La comunidad podría usar las oraciones siguientes en preparación para la Jornada Mundial de la Juventud.

Oración por la Juventud en preparación para la Jornada Mundial de la Juventud

Señor, guíame en el camino de tu amor y permite que sea fiel en la jornada. Con el fuego de tu Espíritu ilumina el camino y ayúdame a levantarme cuando tropiece y caiga.

Hazme un peregrino fiel a tu Palabra de verdad y ayúdame a escoger lo que es recto, justo y verdadero.

Dame de tu amoroso corazón la gracia que necesito para amar a los demás peregrinos y a compartir con ellos tu paz.

Con el poder de tu cruz enséñame a darme en servicio a los pobres y así llenar mi vida de tu amor.

Que de la mesa de tu Palabra y de tu Cuerpo y Sangre, reciba alimento que me llene de vida.

Guía sin peligro mis pasos en tu senda y úneme a todos tus hijos e hijas junto con nuestro Santo Padre y todos aquellos que viajan hacia ti y hacia la vida que nos has prometido. Concédenos esto y todo lo que es bueno por Cristo nuestro Señor.

Amén.

Rev. Austin H. Fleming

Oración por la Juventud (en preparación para la Jornada Mundial de la Juventud)

¿A dónde puedo ir en las tinieblas y cuando tropiezo en el camino?
Iré a la casa del Señor, mi Dios, cuya luz convierte la noche en día.
¿A dónde puedo ir cuando mi corazón sufre y mi espíritu está herido?
¡Iré a la casa del Señor, mi Dios, al Dios que trae alegría a mi juventud!

¿A dónde puedo ir cuando mi corazón lleno, reboza de gratitud y alabanzas?
Iré a la casa del Señor, mi Dios, que con su gracia me da fortaleza.
¿A dónde iré cuando mi corazón está en paz y lleno del espíritu de la verdad?
¡Iré a la casa del Señor, mi Dios, al Dios que trae alegría a mi juventud!

¿A dónde iré a llevar mi entrega a cambio de todo
lo que he recibido?
Iré a la casa del Señor, mi Dios, que me llama a
servir a los necesitados.
¿A dónde iré a dar de mí mismo al igual que Dios
da su amor a todos?
Iré a la casa del Señor, mi Dios, porque su amor
me invita a responder al llamado.
¿A dónde puedo ir para una vida que valga la pena,
a buscar amor que sea fuerte en palabras,
acción y verdad?
¡Iré a la casa del Señor, mi Dios, al Dios que trae
alegría a mi juventud!

Rev. Austin Fleming

Oración de los Padres de los Peregrinos

Señor, has llamado a nuestros hijos a una jornada
de fe y con la ayuda de tu espíritu han
escuchado tu palabra en su corazón y han
respondido.
Haz que sean fieles a tu palabra y protégelos con
tu mano en el viaje a Denver.
Enséñales a escoger la vida y a escoger lo que es
recto, justo y verdadero.
Ayúdales a compartir con otros la vida que tú
prometes, especialmente el servicio a los
pobres.
Abre sus mentes y sus corazones a la verdad de
las escrituras. Aliméntalos con el pan y la copa
de la Eucaristía; y llénalos con amor hacia el
Santo Padre, el Papa Juan Pablo II.
Guía a nuestros jóvenes peregrinos en la senda,
Señor, para que lleguen a ti y a la vida que les
prometes.
Te lo pedimos por Cristo nuestro Señor. Amén.

Rev. Austin H. Fleming

. . . . .

Jóvenes Adultos: Cuando la Vida Está en Tus Manos...

Los jóvenes adultos

La revista "Time", en un estudio sobre los
jóvenes de los Estados Unidos, aparecido en su
número del 12 de julio de 1990, comienza diciendo
que los jóvenes de los 18 a los 29 años "tienen
problemas para tomar decisiones".

Las decisiones con las que se enfrentan estos
jóvenes, son decisiones que van a determinar, en
buena parte, el curso de sus vidas. Conscientes de
esta realidad, José María Pujadas y un grupo de
sacerdotes y religiosas iniciaron en Colombia, en
1968, los "Encuentros de Promoción Juvenil".
Desde el principio se pensó en aquellos jóvenes que
están terminando la escuela superior o que ya están
en la universidad o preparándose para ingresar al
mundo del trabajo.

Metodología de los Encuentros

Valga decir desde un principio que el desarrollo
del Encuentro es similar al desarrollo de los cursillos
de cristiandad, de los que se derivaron. La
metodología del Encuentro, sin embargo, está en
función de los jóvenes adultos, en los momentos en
que están a punto de tomar decisiones que pueden
decidir el resto de sus vidas.

Durante el Encuentro:

1. Al joven se le confronta con su realidad
personal y social: lo que es la juventud "aquí y
ahora". No habrá área en la vida de los jóvenes que
quede sin ser considerada: desde su salud física y
personalidad, hasta sus compromisos de fe, pasando
por su familia e inquietudes profesionales.

2. El Encuentro tiene un fuerte acento vocacional,
en el sentido de que al joven se le va a motivar para
que descubra cuál es el plan que Dios le llama a
realizar en su vida. Para ésto debe aprender a
descubrir sus talentos para poder encaminarlos hacia
la consecución de ese plan.

3. El Encuentro es "descaradamente católico,"
decía José María Pujadas. De hecho, "la
Eucaristía, la Palabra de Dios y la comunidad" son
los tres ejes vivenciales promotores del fin de
semana. A partir de esta experiencia, la vida
adquiere su más auténtico sentido: cerca de Dios y
cerca de la sociedad.

4. El post-encuentro se considera como un
desarrollo lógico de todo el Encuentro: la acción
evangelizadora de los jóvenes dentro de la
comunidad civil y eclesial: "El Encuentro despierta
en los jóvenes y los grupos hambre y sed de
apostolado, buscar planes y organizaciones donde
integrarse a la salida. . .la obra de los Encuentros les
servirá de puente: abrirá el camino y facilitará los
contactos hacia las organizaciones y movimientos
juveniles existentes, especialmente a las parroquias."
(Manual, pág. 36)

5. A lo largo de todo el fin de semana hay una
constante que se expresa de la siguiente manera: tu
vida está en tus manos. Lo que tú no hagas, nadie lo

va a hacer por ti. . . .Existen decisiones en tú vida que sólo tú vas a tener que tomar. . . .

6. Por último, al joven se le introduce, durante el Encuentro, a confrontar su vida con los valores del Evangelio. En la toma de decisiones, no siempre habrá alguien a su lado que le podrá decir lo que tiene que escoger. De ahí que tendrá que desarrollar un profundo sentido moral para hacer sus opciones, inspirado en la certeza de que Jesús representará el héroe que inspira sus acciones, el hermano que camina a su lado, el modelo en la lucha y el portador de la Buena Nueva.

Validez y Versatilidad

Los "Encuentros de Promoción Juvenil" nacieron en Colombia en 1968. De este país se han difundido a otras naciones latinoamericanas. A los Estados Unidos llegaron en 1971 y actualmente se llevan a cabo en Los Angeles, San Diego, Stockton y Oakland, California; Tucson y Nogales, Arizona; y Houston y Dallas, Texas. La versatilidad está en que habiendo sido ideados para jóvenes adultos (de los 18 a los 25 años), el fin de semana y las actividades que derivan de esa experiencia deberían estar animadas por lo que el fundador dice ser una de las metas: "Aspiramos a ser una juventud cristiana creativa, con iniciativa y liderazgo, con sentido y destino en la Historia."

By P. Miguel A. Villegas, MCCJ
Covina, California
Agosto de 1992

· · · · ·

© 1992 WORLD YOUTH DAY, INC

SELECTED USCC RESOURCES

Marketplace Prophets
A highly praised portrayal of 100 years of Catholic social teaching, from the 1891 encyclical, **Rerum Novarum**, to the groups and individuals working for social justice today. "...*The best single presentation on the social teaching of the Catholic Church that I have ever seen.*"- Rev. Thomas H. Stahel, SJ, AMERICA. **Video, 60 minutes,** includes discussion guide. 1991. **No. 427-9, $29.95.**

Heritage and Hope examines present challenges and calls for a recommitment to evangelization. **No. 386-8, 108 pp., $5.95**

On Evangelization in the Modern World
(Evangelii Nuntiandi) Apostolic Exhortation, 1975. **No, 129-6, 70 pp., $4.95**

Catholic Campaign For Children and Families:
A Resource Manual for implementing the statement *Putting Children and Families First*; includes, in addition to the statement, practical planning and support materials. **No. 525-9, 88pp., $4.95** Spanish Resource Manual contains a summary of the statement with discussion guide, planning and support materials, and other resources. **No. 534-8, 48pp., $2.50**

Sr. Thea: Her Own Story celebrates her life as a religious daughter, noted singer, and teacher. Sr. Thea communicated God's love by affirming and cherishing the innate value of each person. **Video, 50 minutes,** includes discussion guide. **No. 491-0, $29.95**

Renewing the Earth
In *An Invitation to Reflection and Action on Environment in Light of Catholic Social Teaching,* the U.S. bishops call on Catholics to reflect on and to discuss environmental problems, including global warming; depletion of the ozone layer; deforestation; and toxic and nuclear waste. 1992. **No. 468-6, 20 pp., $1.95; 50/$90; 100/$165; 500/$675; 1,000/ $1,200.**

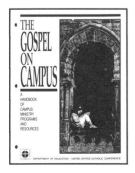

The Gospel on Campus: A Handbook of Campus Ministry Programs and Resources provides a brief history of campus ministry and includes articles on formation, peer ministry, fund raising, ecumenical ministry, and leadership development. **No. 437-6, 216 pp., $14.95**

VISA and MasterCard accepted with phone orders

ORDER FORM - - - WYD

RESOURCES RELATING TO WORLD YOUTH DAY '93

No.	Title	Quantity	Price	Total
525-9	Catholic Campaign for Children & Families		$4.95	
534-8	Catholic Campaign (Spanish Manual)		$2.50	
437-6	The Gospel on Campus		$14.95	
386-8	Heritage and Hope		$5.95	
891-6	The Hispanic Presence		$2.25	
427-9	Marketplace Prophets		$29.95	
199-7	National Plan for Hispanic Ministry		$6.95	
129-6	On Evangelization in the Modern World		$4.95	
825-8	On Human Work		$ 3.95	
959-9	On the Vocation & Mission of the Laity		$2.95	
385-X	Plenty Good Room		$ 9.95	
469-4	Putting Children and Families First		$ 1.95	
	(50/$90; 100/$165; 500/$675)			
468-6	Renewing the Earth		$ 1.95	
	(50/$90; 100/$165; 500/$675; 1000/$1,200)			
491-0	Sr. Thea: Her Own Story		$29.95	
470-8	A Time for Remembering, Reconciling....		$1.95	
	(50/$90; 100/$165; 500/$675)			
528-3	A Year of Preparation: Resource Manual		$5.95	
171-7	Young Adult Ministry Resources		$ 5.95	

Subtotal _____

Postage and Handling + _____

GRAND TOTAL _____

USCC Publishing Services
3211 Fourth Street, N.E.,
Washington, D.C. 20017-1194

Name _____

Phone ( ) _____

Organization _____

Office/Department _____

Street Address _____
(Not P.O. Box)

City _____State _____Zip _____

USCC Account # _____
(if applicable)

Postage and Handling	
$10.00 and Under	$ 2.25
$ 10.01 - $ 25.00	$ 3.25
$ 25.01 - $ 50.00	$ 4.25
$ 50.01 - $ 100.00	$ 6.25
$ 100.01 - $ 500.00	$10.00
$ 500.01 - $1,000.00	$15.00
Over $1,000.00	3% of total order

Call toll-free 1-800-235-8722 or FAX 1-301-209-0016

Be Prepared!

Continue your celebration of World Youth Day.

Order now!

World Youth Day Manual '94

This manual will facilitate your ongoing plans to expand the experience of pilgrimage. Directors of Religious Education, Campus Ministry, Youth Ministry and Young Adult Ministry, and all pastoral leaders concerned with outreach to today's youth will find the resources you seek to continue developing your programs of evangelization and service.

No. 533-X Prepublication price $6.95

Please send me _____ copies of World Youth Day '94 at $6.95 each

USCC Publishing Services
3211 Fourth Street, N.E.,
Washington, D.C. 20017-1194

Subtotal _____
Postage and Handling + _____
GRAND TOTAL _____

Name_____
Phone ( )_____
Organization_____
Office/Department_____
Street Address_____
(Not P.O. Box)

City_____ State_____ Zip_____

USCC Account #_____
(if applicable)

Postage and Handling

$10.00 and Under	$ 2.25
$ 10.01 - $ 25.00	$ 3.25
$ 25.01 - $ 50.00	$ 4.25
$ 50.01 - $ 100.00	$ 6.25
$ 100.01 - $ 500.00	$10.00
$ 500.01 - $1,000.00	$15.00
Over $1,000.00	3% of total order

To order:
- **Call Toll-Free 1-800-235-USCC (8722). Mastercard and VISA accepted.**
- **FAX your order to 1-301-209-0016.**
- **Fold this card over and mail in, using the address on the reverse.**
  (Please do not staple this card.)

USCC Publishing Services
3211 Fourth Street, N.E.,
Washington, D.C. 20017-1194